ASHE Higher Education Report: Volume 32
Kelly Ward, Lisa E. Wolf-Wendel, Series Editors

Community College Faculty: Overlooked and Undervalued

Barbara K. Townsend
Susan B. Twombly

Community College Faculty: Overlooked and Undervalued
Barbara K. Townsend and Susan B. Twombly
ASHE Higher Education Report: Volume 32, Number 6
Kelly Ward, Lisa E. Wolf-Wendel, Series Editors

ISSN 1551-6970   electronic ISSN 1554-6306   ISBN 978-0-7879-9777-9

The ASHE Higher Education Report is part of the Jossey-Bass Higher and Adult Education Series and is published six times a year by Wiley Subscription Services, Inc., A Wiley Company, at Jossey-Bass, 989 Market Street, San Francisco, California 94103-1741.

For subscription information, see the Back Issue/Subscription Order Form in the back of this volume.

CALL FOR PROPOSALS: Prospective authors are strongly encouraged to contact Kelly Ward (kaward@wsu.edu) or Lisa Wolf-Wendel (lwolf@ku.edu). See "About the ASHE Higher Education Report Series" in the back of this volume.

Visit the Jossey-Bass Web site at **www.josseybass.com.**

Printed in the United States of America on acid-free recycled paper.

Advisory Board

The ASHE Higher Education Report Series is sponsored by the Association for the Study of Higher Education (ASHE), which provides an editorial advisory board of ASHE members.

Contents

Executive Summary

Public community colleges in the United States enroll approximately 6 million students and employ nearly four hundred thousand full- and part-time faculty to teach them. Annually, these faculty members serve millions of students, many of whom are first-generation, low-income, minority, and older students with varying levels of academic preparation.

Despite their large numbers and the importance of the role community college faculty members play, relatively little is known about them. When they are studied, they are often examined through lenses more appropriate for faculty in four-year colleges and universities. In this comparison, community college faculty fare particularly poorly, as the majority do not hold Ph.D.s, teaching is their primary function, they teach lower-level courses, and they have little control over who their students are.

A Profile of Community College Faculty

Roughly one-third of all community college faculty are full time; this third teaches more than half of all credit courses. Demographically, full-time faculty members are overwhelmingly white (80 percent) and middle-aged (an average age of fifty). African Americans make up 6.9 percent of the full-time faculty, Hispanics only 5.9 percent. These percentages are lower than expected, given the diversity of the community college student population and the fact that individuals can become faculty members with the master's degree. On the other hand, women are well represented, constituting half of all full-time faculty, much higher than at any other institutional type. Women in particular find the community college a good place to teach while balancing family responsibilities. The typical educational credential for full-time community college faculty members is the master's degree. Perhaps as a result, the average annual salary of community college faculty is about $53,000, compared with an average salary of $60,000 in comprehensive colleges and universities and $74,000 in research universities.

Part-time faculty currently constitute approximately two-thirds of the teaching force in community colleges. They provide flexibility at lower cost to the institution. Demographically, part-time faculty members are remarkably similar to their full-time counterparts: 50 percent female, 16 percent minority, and somewhat younger. They make little money.

Faculty Work in the Context of the Community College

Faculty work is conditioned by the community college's mission. Committed to open access and the success of students, community colleges are often portrayed as teaching colleges. Their faculty spend most of their time engaged in classroom teaching and related activities such as advising and curriculum development. Despite the fact that teaching is the primary activity of community college faculty members, some scholars challenge the assumption that teaching is highly valued.

Becoming a community college faculty member may not be a person's initial career goal but rather may result from viewing the position as a positive choice after working in other settings, whether inside or outside academe. Those who consciously intend to become community college faculty members will find that no official preparation is required, other than receipt of the appropriate academic credential required for entry, which, depending on one's broad teaching area, may be a master's degree with eighteen hours in the teaching field or a baccalaureate degree or less in career and technical education fields.

Faculty work is greatly influenced by institutional mission and a variety of internal and external factors. In general, it appears that administrators still retain considerable control over faculty work in community colleges.

Collective bargaining and participation in faculty governance are the two most common ways for faculty to circumscribe administrative authority, but even these two institutional features have their limitations.

Much more needs to be known about the process by which faculty members are recruited and hired, as age data suggest that there will be constant demand for faculty in the future. What we do know suggests that the search process resembles the search process in other types of colleges and universities.

Looking to the Future: The Status of Community College Teaching as a Profession

Whether or not community college teaching is a profession is a question that has driven much of the early two-year college discourse about those who teach at community colleges. Community college teaching evidences some characteristics of a profession, but not all. We view community college teaching as a profession that finds itself in a middle position on the continuum of teaching as a profession between high school and university teaching. It occupies this middle position not because of weaknesses of the community college or the individuals occupying faculty positions but because of the characteristics and role of the community college and its students.

Several current and future factors influence the professional identity of the community college professoriate. A major one is the development of what has been termed "the community college baccalaureate," a bachelor's degree awarded by the community college. As more community colleges are authorized to award this degree, required entry credentials for community college faculty members may change, as may expectations of them to be scholars (defined as those who contribute to the knowledge base of their teaching area). Entry credentials for career and technical education faculty may also be raised as more students with the A.A.S. degree, traditionally a nontransfer degree, seek transfer to four-year schools.

The conception of the community college as *nouveau college,* an institution less focused on student access and success and more focused on its place in the market, may also influence the professional role of community college faculty.

A major challenge to the professional status of the community college professoriate is the high percentage of part-time faculty members. Although the reasons for their extensive use are varied, the major one is cost savings, as the low cost of a community college education compared with other educational institutions is one of the major reasons for its high enrollments. It is therefore unlikely that the percentage of part-time faculty will decline much in the coming decades. Perhaps what needs to be addressed is ways to increase the professionalism of part-time faculty without detracting from that of full-time faculty members. It is this group of faculty who need to take a greater role in governance to ensure they have sufficient control over conditions affecting their work roles, including the use of technology in teaching and pressures to participate in economic development activities.

A Fresh Look at Community College Faculty

For much of the late twentieth century, discourse about the community college posited it as an alternative institution, outside the mainstream of higher education institutions, in marked contrast to the university, and with a substantially lower status in the academic hierarchy.

The standard or stereotypical definition of a faculty member as someone who conducts research, teaches, and participates in disciplinary and institutional service is inadequate and inappropriate for the community college of the twenty-first century. Inevitably, application of this standard definition has led to the perception that anyone whose faculty position does not include all three roles is somehow a lesser or inferior faculty member. This standard definition of faculty roles is inappropriate when viewing the work of community college faculty members.

Teaching is clearly the centerpiece of faculty work in community colleges and so it should remain. Although teaching is the agreed-upon emphasis of the community college, there is considerable evidence that teaching is not given the attention it deserves, given its primary place in the community college. We believe the scholarship of teaching undergirds all the work of faculty in the community college. Although most may not articulate participation in this kind of scholarship, it is what they intuitively do as they prepare for classes and seek to engage students in learning.

We have identified several challenges to understanding community college faculty members—relatively little research on community college faculty members, limited scope of existing published studies, and the horizontal nature of scholarship (tendency to study the same topic in multiple sites)—and areas needing further scholarship—the job search and community college faculty labor market; the tenure and promotion process; faculty work life for minority and women faculty; occupational, career, and technical education faculty; Ph.D. graduates who take community college faculty positions immediately out of graduate school; part-time faculty members; and shared governance. Above all, we need more research on the process by which newly hired faculty members, both full and part time, are socialized into and learn the values, roles, and responsibilities of community college faculty members. Our goal is that all readers will come to view community college faculty members as colleagues making a distinct contribution to their students and to faculty work. Such an understanding is critical in the current policy environment that values postsecondary education for everyone.

Foreword

The community college professoriate is a misunderstood segment of the American higher education system. As this monograph clearly demonstrates, community college faculty are both understudied and underappreciated. The orientation of existing research is limited and primarily compares community college faculty members with their counterparts at four-year institutions. Such comparisons normalize the experiences and expectations of four-year college and university faculty, resulting in unfair portrayals of community college faculty as somehow inferior.

This monograph addresses these limitations by painting a more nuanced and thoughtful portrait of community college faculty, their profession, and the context in which they work. The monograph contributes significantly to the field by reviewing key literature on community college faculty members and providing a framework for understanding the nature of their profession, factors that have shaped their responsibilities, and emerging trends (such as the community college baccalaureate) that will affect community college faculty in the future.

The authors have constructed an exemplary analysis of faculty careers that helps the reader understand community college faculty at a critical time in the development of the community college. The authors also provide much needed attention to the historical roots of contemporary faculty experiences and provide an overview of the key dimensions of faculty careers—from graduate preparation to retirement. The authors' concluding discussion about the extent to which community college faculty fit with traditional definitions of professions is particularly thoughtful and illuminating.

This monograph will be useful to prospective and current community college faculty, community college administrators, and scholars who study higher education. In particular the monograph compels scholars to engage in research that enhances our understanding of the nature of the community college faculty experience in and of itself and not simply in terms of how it differs from what might be expected at universities and four-year colleges.

Lisa E. Wolf-Wendel
Series Editor

Acknowledgments

We would like to thank the University of Missouri–Columbia for funding a Big 12 faculty development leave for Barbara so that she could spend a week in Lawrence, Kansas, working with Susan on the monograph. We would also like to thank the three anonymous reviewers for their helpful comments on the first draft.

 Published online in Wiley InterScience
(www.interscience.wiley.com) • DOI: 10.1002/aehe.3206

Overview

WITH ROOTS STRETCHING BACK TO the late nineteenth
century, two-year colleges in the United States appear in the twenty-
first century primarily as community colleges, defined as public higher
education institutions whose highest degree offering has traditionally been the
associate degree. In 2003–04, almost twelve hundred community colleges
enrolled 7.6 million credit-bearing students. That same year community
colleges enrolled approximately 40 percent of all undergraduate students,
including 46 percent of all Hispanic students, 45 percent of all American
Indian students, and 44 percent of African American students (Horn and
Nevill, 2006).

In 2005 public degree-granting two-year schools employed a total of
354,300 full-time and part-time faculty members, according to data from the
fall 2005 Integrated Postsecondary Education Data System (IPEDS) staff
survey (Keller, 2006). Put another way, 43 percent of all full- and part-time
faculty members work in community colleges. Despite this fact, community
college faculty are overlooked and undervalued. As a 1998 report from
the National Center for Postsecondary Improvement stated, "Community
college faculty receive scant attention from postsecondary researchers—or
worse, are simply dismissed as a separate, and by implication lesser, class of
college professors" (p. 43).

A 2004 issue of *Change: The Magazine of Higher Learning,* illustrates well
the overlooked and undervalued nature of community college faculty. The
entire issue is devoted to the "perfect storm" in which community colleges
find themselves. George Boggs, president and chief executive officer of the
American Association of Community Colleges, notes in the lead article that
community colleges are being expected to do more at the same time that state

---

funding is declining, thus necessitating tuition increases. Other authors in this special issue address the topics of access, quality, policy, transfers, assessment, civic engagement, diversity programs, and the knotty question of who will lead community colleges. In fifty-eight pages focusing on community colleges, not one author mentions in more than passing the faculty who teach in these colleges. For institutions claiming to be teaching and learning centered, this lack of attention to those who teach there is astounding. Leaders are needed, quality must be defined, and transfer policies must be in place, but the hundreds of thousands of faculty daily facing classes full of students who have poured through the open doors are seemingly forgotten. They are marginalized in this particular examination of community colleges and in the community college literature more generally.

Why is it important to know about faculty? In four-year institutions, it is a common cliché that faculty are the heart of an institution, lasting much longer as organizational members than do students and typically longer than many top-level administrators. The same is true for community colleges although less frequently acknowledged. Monroe (1977) wrote in a textbook about the community college that "after the student, the most important element in the community college is the faculty" (p. 245). Certainly it is faculty who provide the instruction that students seek, facilitating their access to four-year colleges and universities or directly to a variety of careers. A profile of who community college faculty members are and what they do enables policymakers and faculty members in other institutional settings to understand the parameters under which community college faculty function, including institutional mission, nature of the student body, and role expectations.

Conversely, lack of knowledge about community college faculty results in reliance on portraits of community colleges and their faculties derived from a comparison with four-year college faculty, an inappropriate comparison that typically leaves community college faculty found wanting. For example, Caplow and McGee (1958) in their pathbreaking study referred to community colleges as being the "bush league." Likewise, one of the more recent pictures of community college faculty as professionals comes from Clark's classic study, *Small Worlds, Different Worlds* (1987). In this study, community college faculty members are viewed as being more nearly like high school teachers in terms of control over their work than like higher education faculty members. These depictions of community colleges and those who teach in them have shaped generations of thinking about the academic hierarchy and consequently scholarly thinking about faculty work in community colleges.

Thus at best, community college faculty are ignored in literature about faculty and at worst, the literature perpetuates negative stereotypes about them. Many four-year faculty members may have only these stereotypes in mind and may know only that some of the students at the four-year institution go to a nearby community college to take courses to fulfill general education requirements. When viewed by faculty members with doctorates who work at "real" colleges and universities, these courses may be considered to be "easier" courses than ones taught at the four-year level. This perception exists partly because the courses are apt to be taught by faculty without a doctorate; consequently, these faculty may be perceived as less qualified and knowledgeable about the course content than are four-year faculty. Although the percentage of community college faculty members with doctorates continues to creep up, the negative stereotypes about the quality of community colleges and their faculties is slow to change.

This lack of information about community college faculty members is problematic because, as mentioned earlier, they teach almost 40 percent of all undergraduates and, in particular, a high percentage of students of color. Many of the students whom they teach transfer to four-year colleges at some point. And many students starting at four-year colleges have taken, while still in high school, dual-credit or dual-enrollment classes offered by community colleges; these students then "transfer" those courses to the four-year schools where they matriculate. Additionally, many four-year college students concurrently enroll in two-year colleges or attend them during the summer to facilitate their attaining a baccalaureate. In the twenty-first century educational swirl, an increasing number of four-year college graduates take courses at community colleges as part of their baccalaureate education (Townsend, 2001). Knowing about the faculty members who instruct these courses may help to allay the fears of faculty at four-year colleges and universities that such courses are weaker. These fears can sometimes result in a reluctance to accept dual- or concurrent-enrollment courses taught by community college faculty, a condescending attitude toward community college courses taken in the summer and through concurrent enrollment, and a disinterest in admitting two-year college transfer students.

Most research about faculty has been on faculty in four-year institutions, typically research institutions. No standard work exists on community college faculty that mirrors Bowen and Schuster's *American Professors: A Natural Resource Imperiled* (1986), Finkelstein, Seal, and Schuster's *The New Academic Generation: A Profession in Transformation* (1998), and Schuster and Finkelstein's *The American Faculty: The Restructuring of Academic Work and Careers* (2006). Although these authors mention community college faculty, their work is clearly focused on faculty in four-year institutions. In these books frameworks used to understand four-year college faculty are often assumed to apply to community college faculty. When applied, however, the frameworks such as those used by Burton Clark in *Academic Life: Small Worlds, Different Worlds* (1987) suggest that community college faculty are deficient when compared with their four-year counterparts, especially those at research universities whose academic lives set the norm for all faculty.

To complicate the matter, most of the research that does exist on community college faculty appears in journals specific to the community college world, journals not typically read by those outside the community college. Some research also appears in other venues with limited distribution such as dissertations or institutional reports, further restricting what is known about community colleges and their faculties.

In the past decade, three books have helped provide a portrait of specific aspects of community college faculty work life: Grubb and Associates' *Honored but Invisible* (1999), Outcalt's *A Profile of the Community College Professorate, 1975–2000* (2002b), and Levin, Kater, and Wagoner's *Community College Faculty: At Work in the New Economy* (2006). Grubb and Associates (1999) offer valuable, often critical, insight into the work lives of community college faculty through their qualitative look at arts and science and occupational-technical faculty in thirty-two community colleges across the nation. Outcalt (2002b) uses descriptive data from a national survey of faculty to explore issues of professionalization among the community college professoriate. Through both quantitative and qualitative means, Levin, Kater, and Wagoner (2006) examine community college faculty members' roles as managed professionals in the globalized economy. Seidman's previous work (1985) and the more recent books of London (1978), Cohen and Brawer (1977), and Garrison (1967), serve a very important function in helping us understand specific aspects of community college faculty. We also note that Cohen and Brawer's *The American Community College* (2003), now in its fourth edition, continues to be the standard reference on community colleges. Although these authors consider faculty an important topic, it is just one of many they cover. None of the books referenced above offer a comprehensive synthesis of what is currently known about these individuals and the conditions of their work.

Our goal in this volume is to provide a broad overview of the community college faculty in the early twenty-first century. Our focus is limited to the faculty at public community colleges and does not include the faculty at private two-year colleges or at for-profit schools that are two years or less in programmatic scope. We also have limited our focus to the work of community college faculty, meaning what they do in the context of the community college, not how they do it (for example, using instructional technology). At times we explain certain dimensions of the community college such as its missions and the nature of its student body or institutional approaches to governance, including unionization. We usually do not provide examples from specific institutions, and we do not present best practices. The community college literature is replete with this kind of information, which would be impossible to synthesize in one volume.

In preparing our overview, we sought literature about the community college professoriate, with particular emphasis on peer-reviewed articles, chapters, and books published in the last ten to fifteen years. To find many of the peer-reviewed articles on faculty, we searched the two major scholarly journals about community colleges (*Community College Journal of Research and Practice* and *Community College Review*) and the three major general higher education journals (*Journal of Higher Education, Research in Higher Education,* and *The Review of Higher Education*). We set the time period of

January 1990 through June 2006 as part of our search parameters so as to examine relatively current articles. Believing a historical perspective is important, we examined earlier issues of *Community College Journal,* the publication of the American Association of Community Colleges. This organization represents almost all two-year colleges and since 1930 has published a journal that focuses on issues of interest to its members. Thus the journal has published and continues to do so articles on issues of concern to two-year college leaders and faculty over many decades. In addition to *Community College Journal,* several current peer-reviewed journals focus on community colleges. The best-known ones—*Community College Journal of Research and Practice* and *Community College Review*—serve as major outlets for scholarship about the community college. Many of the studies we reviewed are from these two journals. We also drew heavily on the three recent, already named books about various aspects of community college faculty's lives (Grubb and Associates, 1999; Levin, Kater, and Wagoner, 2006; Outcalt, 2002b), as well as chapters from older texts and from Cohen and Brawer's *The American Community College* (2003). One noticeable absence from our review is dissertations. We decided to focus only on published work that had been submitted externally for some sort of vetting. This literature forms public understanding of community college faculty and their work. In addition, review of dissertations would have been an enormous undertaking beyond the scope of this work.

In reviewing this literature, we faced several challenges in our effort to generalize about community college faculty. First of all, faculty work conditions depend on several factors such as an individual's employment status (full or part time, tenure track, tenured, or off track) and union status (member of a faculty union, nonmember from choice or lack of opportunity). Even if all the faculty members in a particular study are classified as full-time instructional, they may not teach but rather may be assigned to other instructional activities such as librarianship or counseling. When they are included in a study, their attitudes may be different from those of faculty members who are full-time teachers. Yet studies of faculty attitudes do not always distinguish among different groups of faculty.

Another difficulty is the limited scope of many studies of community college faculty. Other than a recent spate of studies that use data from one of the National Study of Postsecondary Faculty (NSOPF) surveys in 1993, 1999, or 2004; the Carnegie survey (on which Huber based her 1998 monograph); and national studies conducted through the Higher Education Research Institute at UCLA, most quantitative faculty studies published in community college journals are small in scope. They are typically single-institution or possibly regional studies. Additionally, researchers have tended to focus on community colleges in a few states such as California, Florida, and Illinois, states with well-developed, extensive community college systems. Faculty members in these states have more frequently been the focus of research than have been faculty members in states with a smaller number of community colleges or no graduate programs focusing on community colleges. Given the tremendous differences among states in mission emphasis, funding, and opportunities for faculty unionization, it is likely that institutional differences play a more important role than is sometimes apparent in studies of faculty work life.

Finally, in considering what we report in this monograph, one must understand who typically does research on community college faculty members. Unlike research on four-year college and university faculty members, which is done by faculty members in those settings, it is faculty members in four-year universities who do much of the published research on community college faculty. To be sure, many of these individuals have worked at one time in community colleges, although others have not. These others are outsiders in the sense that they have not worked at community colleges even if they teach about them. Both groups bring a distanced perspective, a situation that has both pros and cons. The benefits of the outsider view include seeing the institution and its faculty members with a fresh, and sometimes critical, eye that is often lacking in the almost missionary writing about community colleges characteristic of the 1970s and 1980s. Grubb and Associates' *Honored but Invisible* is a good example of a sympathetic outsider seeing community college teaching and those who do it with a fresh, unclouded look. On the other hand, they may inadvertently bring a four-year perspective to their work.

To increase understanding about community college faculty members and an appreciation of what they do, we focus in this volume on the five major topics described below.

"A Profile of Community College Faculty" relies on data from the various iterations of the National Survey of Postsecondary Faculty and other sources to paint a demographic profile of today's community college faculty, both full time and part time. ("Part time" is the term we use for those who are not full-time faculty at the community college but still teach there.)

"Faculty Work in the Context of the Community College" discusses the extent of their participation in the three traditional faculty roles of teaching, research, and service, given the parameters of community college missions and students. A discussion of literature about professional development in included, as it is a means to help faculty in their institutional roles. The chapter also looks at the job satisfaction of community college faculty and the likelihood of their leaving the institution.

"Dimensions of the Community College Faculty Career" includes a review of the literature on salient dimensions of the faculty career, including career paths to becoming a full-time community college faculty member and career paths once at the community college, taking into consideration tenure, promotion, and salary.

"Institutional Factors Affecting Community College Faculty Work Life" focuses on the role of faculty institutional associations and unions in governance, and departmental organization.

"Looking to the Future: The Status of Community College Teaching as a Profession" includes a discussion of the concepts of professions and professionalization, reviews perspectives on whether community college teaching is a profession, and speculates about the effects on a professionalized faculty of selected emerging issues facing the community college.

"A Fresh Look at Community College Faculty" presents examples of university professors' discourse about the community college to illustrate how it casts the institution as marginalized and thus its faculty members as marginalized members of the professoriate. Given recent developments in community college curricular offerings, we question the appropriateness of this discourse. We then indicate challenges in understanding community college faculty members and suggest some areas of research that would increase our knowledge about these individuals.

A final chapter includes several conclusions we have drawn about community college faculty, based on the existing literature.

We hope this monograph, devoted to the essential aspects of community college faculty life, will serve several purposes. First, by its very publication, we seek to reduce the marginality of community college faculty members in literature about the professoriate. Next, we intend for this monograph to provide useful information for those considering a career as a community college faculty member. We also hope this in-depth look at community college faculty will aid in identifying commonalities and differences in faculty work life across institutional sectors and thus provide new ways to view community college faculty, not as deviations from the norm but as colleagues making a distinctive contribution to their students and to faculty work. Such an understanding is critical in the current policy environment that values seamless movement of students among educational sectors, including from the two-year to the four-year sector.

Our intended audience is twofold: current and prospective community college faculty, and scholars of the community college. Both groups seek to understand the nature of the community college professoriate and how it is similar to and different from that of faculty members at certain types of four-year schools, especially research universities. The chapters on the nature of faculty work and dimensions of the faculty career may be of the most interest to prospective faculty members, as these chapters describe the work and career trajectory of the community college professoriate. Scholars should find the entire review of the literature helpful in future research and may be particularly interested in the chapter that nests discussion of community college faculty in the concepts of professions and professionalism and in the final chapter in which we draw some conclusions for research and practice.

A Profile of Community College Faculty

A S OF FALL 2003, 43 percent of all faculty members in public, nonprofit higher education institutions were in public community colleges (*Chronicle of Higher Education Almanac,* 2004–05). In this chapter, we provide a demographic profile of these faculty members. Demographic data about community college faculty come from various sources, each using somewhat different data collected in different years. This chapter attempts to piece together these data to provide as accurate a picture of the community college professoriate as possible. Further, acknowledging the reality that two-thirds of community college faculty members are part time (Cataldi, Fahimi, and Bradburn, 2005), we break this profile into two parts. First we examine selected characteristics of the full-time faculty and some research about these characteristics and then we turn to the growing cadre of part-time faculty members.

Full-Time Faculty

In describing community college faculty members who are full-time faculty, we shall look at race/ethnicity, gender, age, teaching area, and salaries.

Race and Ethnicity

An overwhelming majority (80 percent) of full-time community college faculty members are white. According to the NSOPF:04 data, African Americans make up 6.9 percent of all full-time two-year college faculty members, while Hispanics comprise 5.9 percent (Cataldi, Fahimi, and

Bradburn, 2005). Data from the fall 2005 IPEDS Staff Survey show a similar picture. According to the IPEDS data set, 82 percent of full-time faculty members at public two-year, degree-granting colleges are white, with almost 7 percent black non-Hispanic and almost 5 percent Hispanic. Asian or Pacific Islanders account for almost 4 percent, American Indian or Alaska Natives less than 1 percent (Keller, 2006). Another way of viewing these findings is to ask what percentage of all African American professors work at community colleges. According to 1998 U.S. Department of Education data (Manzo, 2000), approximately 25 percent of all black professors work at a community college.

Given the high percentage of minority students attending public two-year colleges (46 percent of all Hispanic students, 45 percent of all American Indian students, and 44 percent of African American students in 2003–04, according to Horn and Nevill, 2006), it is surprising and disappointing that the percentage of full-time minority faculty members is not higher. Community colleges would seem to be perfectly positioned to hire faculty of color, especially those colleges located in urban areas. Close to half of all community college faculty are expected to retire within the decade (Rifkin, 2000), thus opening up positions for new hires, including faculty of color. Additionally, the educational credential required to become a faculty member teaching academic or transfer courses is a master's degree. Nearly seventy thousand (13.5 percent) of all master's degrees awarded in 2002–03 were earned by African Americans and Hispanics (*Chronicle of Higher Education Almanac,* 2005), so a pool of minorities is available who could potentially fill community college faculty slots.

As Manzo (2000) noted after interviewing several individuals, faculty positions in community colleges would seemingly hold great appeal for faculty of color. Some minority faculty members are drawn to the institution because of its mission of open access and its emphasis on teaching. "Drawn by the diversity of the student body, the employment opportunities and the potential for gaining experience in the classroom, many professors of color begin their higher education careers at two-year colleges" (Manzo, 2000, p. 54). Yet as appealing as the community college might be to faculty of color, they may find themselves drawn to four-year institutions because of their higher salaries and lighter teaching responsibilities (Manzo, 2000). Manzo notes that even though Prince George's Community College in Largo, Maryland, has a 70 percent minority student body, is located near urban areas, and has made a sustained effort to hire minority faculty, it has not made the gains it would like in diversifying its faculty. Manzo attributes some of the problem to a lack of qualified candidates as well as competition with other colleges and universities that also have engaged in efforts to recruit faculty of color.

For more than a decade, suggestions have been made about ways to recruit more community college faculty of color, including recruiting them while they are still in graduate programs, placing ads in media targeted to minorities, and including minorities on search committees (Opp and Smith, 1994; Owens, Reis, and Hall, 1994). Opp and Gosetti (2002) suggest another way is by increasing the number of women administrators of color. According to the authors, the greater the percentage of female administrators of color at a two-year school, the greater the likelihood of its having "an increase in its proportional representation of women full-time faculty of color" (p. 620). Some four-year colleges and universities have taken a "grow your own" approach. This approach would seemingly be harder in community colleges, as prospective faculty members have to attend other institutions to earn the requisite entrance degrees—but it might not be impossible.

We know very little about the experiences of faculty members of color in community colleges. One study used a national data set on community college faculty and supplemented it with focus group interviews to discuss what campus life is like for community college faculty members of color (Bower, 2002). Analysis of the survey data indicated little variation in the responses of minority and majority faculty members about such things as workload and perceptions of the institution. Minority faculty members who were surveyed, however, were less likely to believe that claims of discriminatory practice are highly exaggerated. Through focus groups with minority instructors in three Florida community colleges, Bower found that "some minority community college faculty continue to feel that race or ethnicity influences their interactions with colleagues and students" (p. 82). These faculty members believe that racial or ethnic discrimination exists at their institution, yet they did "express general satisfaction with their professional lives" (p. 86).

Gender

Women who are full-time community college faculty members currently receive far more scholarly attention than do faculty members of color, perhaps because the percentage of women who teach in community colleges is so high. Depending on the data source, women represent between 49 percent (Cataldi, Fahimi, and Bradburn, 2005) and 52 percent (Keller, 2006) of full-time faculty members in the community college. The community college has the highest percentage of female full-time faculty members of any institutional type. Women have made dramatic inroads into the community college professoriate over the last forty years, rising from 25.1 percent of the total in 1969 to 33.4 percent in 1984 to 44.2 percent in 1992 (Schuster and Finkelstein, 2006) to approximately 50 percent currently.

Scholarship about these women typically focuses on their fit and treatment in the institution. Two general themes or perspectives are reflected in this literature. One is that academic life for women in community colleges is good and that it is better than in four-year colleges and universities. The other is that the high percentage of women in community colleges reflects women's marginalization in academe.

A number of recent studies highlight the advantages for women of holding a faculty position in a community college. One significant benefit is the perceived ability to balance career and family more easily than in a four-year college or university with high expectations for research. In a survey of women full-time faculty in some of the Chicago city colleges, Townsend (1998) asked respondents whether they chose to work at a two-year college or would prefer to work at a four-year college. The majority responded that teaching at the community college was preferable because doing so "enables them comfortably to achieve professional fulfillment, sometimes combined with raising a family" (Townsend, 1998, p. 660). Although university scholars may denigrate teaching at community colleges and view their faculty as marginal in the professoriate, "for many women faculty, teaching full-time in a two-year college is the ideal employment," because it enables them to "combine having a career with raising families" (Townsend, 1995, p. 42). In other words, many women purposefully *choose* to teach at a community college rather than being consigned to one because they could not find employment at a four-year college.

Although many women faculty members have indicated they teach at a community college partly because doing so enables them to balance career and family, only Wolf-Wendel, Ward, and Twombly (2007) have examined how they do so and what institutional factors affect these efforts. The authors interviewed thirty women from twelve community colleges; each was a full-time faculty member in her probationary period, either for tenure or a long-term contract. All the women had children and almost all were married. None taught in technical or career education programs. The researchers found that most of the women consciously chose to teach at the community college, following work experience in other settings, including other higher education institutions. Because they had worked elsewhere, they could appreciate the advantages of the community college as a work environment. Many were influenced by their love of teaching and by "a social justice commitment to teaching at the community college level." As in the Townsend (1998) study, some women also did not want to teach at four-year institutions because doing so seemed to entail too much sacrifice of family time and personal life and because of pressures to publish.

As positive as the women in Wolf-Wendel, Ward, and Twombly's study (2007) were about teaching in the community college, they were stressed not only by efforts to combine family and work but also by the work itself. It was time consuming and "hard work." Being in a probationary period added to their stress because there was some concern they might not "pass." Wolf-Wendel, Ward, and Twombly's study (2007) may be the first one that documents and addresses community college faculty members' concerns about the probationary period. Most scholarship assumes that tenure or long-term contracts in the two-year college are granted almost automatically and little stress is associated with the process.

Wolf-Wendel, Ward, and Twombly's study (2007) is also groundbreaking because it documents the frustrations of women community college faculty members who have given birth and are contemplating having other children. As with women faculty in the four-year sector, some concern exists that attention to their family might be perceived as not caring sufficiently about their work and that having another child should be deferred until the probationary period is over. Occasionally a woman complained about lack of a supportive institutional environment for women faculty with young children—suspicion that women working from home are not putting in sufficient hours or policies prohibiting faculty from bringing their children to the office. Despite these complaints and frustrations, the women believed that "being a parent and being a professor at a community college are compatible roles" and that the balance they had created between work and family "would not have been possible if they were faculty members at a four-year institution." Although the women perceived their situation to be a relatively good one for combining work and family, the community college itself did little to intentionally facilitate the situation of women faculty with children, according to the researchers.

Studies that focus on faculty in general or sometimes just on two-year college faculty may provide insight into faculty members' perceptions of institutional treatment or attitudes toward female faculty and sometimes minority faculty members. For example, Huber (1998) asked in her national study of faculty attitudes and trends whether "female and minority faculty are treated fairly" (p. 8) at the respondent's institution. Responses were categorized by type of institution, with faculty at associate of arts colleges having the highest percentage of female faculty (85 percent) and minority faculty (82 percent) agreeing "strongly" or "somewhat" that female and minority faculty are treated fairly at their institution (Table 126). A few years later Hagedorn and Laden (2002) examined responses to selected questions from a different national survey of community college faculty to answer the general question "Is there a chilly climate at community colleges for women faculty?" (p. 70). Their analysis indicated that men and white faculty were more apt than women and faculty of color to agree with the statement "Claims of discriminatory practices against women and minorities have been greatly exaggerated" (p. 75).

Perna (2003) devoted an entire study to the status of women and minority community college faculty members. Using NSOPF:93 data, she drew on several perspectives about the labor market, including human capital theory, to develop a "conceptual model for exploring sex and race/ethnic group differences in several employment outcomes" (p. 209) among two-year college faculty at public institutions. Including both full- and part-time faculty members and tenure status of regular faculty, she found differences in various dimensions of the "employment experiences of women and minorities" (p. 234). First, she noted that women and men are virtually equally likely to hold the rank of instructor (42 percent of community college full-time faculty members in the 1993 NSOPF data). Among the 45 percent of full-time faculty reporting a rank of assistant, associate, or full professor, however, women were less likely to hold the rank of full professor (15 percent) than men (23 percent). (The fact that fewer women and minorities are full professors could be accounted for "after taking into account differences in human capital, structural, and market characteristics" [p. 225].) In fact, female part-time faculty had higher average salaries than did male part-time faculty. Regarding possible ethnic differences, she concluded that the "general absence of observed racial/ethnic group differences in several types of employment experiences for faculty at public 2-year colleges suggests an absence of racial/ethnic inequality" (p. 238). She cautioned, however, that more must be done "to correct the continued under representation of faculty of color at these institutions" (p. 238).

The other, more critical view of women in community colleges takes the perspective that the community college's high percentage of women who are faculty members is evidence of these faculty members' marginalization in academe (Townsend, 1995). Although it is true that women are hired in great numbers, the fact that women represent such a high percentage of the faculty only in the lowest-tier postsecondary institution is evidence of women's, and the community college's, marginalization in academe. Even Wolf-Wendel, Ward, and Twombly (2007), while positive overall about the experience of women faculty members in community colleges, express some regret that women who want to balance work and family feel as if they have to seek work in community colleges. Although unstated, one implication is that they are missing out on working in a higher-status place. And although male faculty are also perceived to be marginalized in academe because of working in community colleges (see Townsend and LaPaglia, 2000), the issue of faculty marginalization has been more frequently addressed for women faculty members, perhaps because women have historically been viewed as marginalized in society.

Not everyone accepts this view. For example, Townsend (1998) argues, "University faculty who consider employment in the community college as evidence of the marginalization of women as academics are evaluating the employment in terms of their own professional values. By positing community college teaching as inferior employment, they diminish the achievements of the many women who find employment in the community college satisfactory or even ideal" (p. 661).

Cohen and Brawer (1987) appear to be among the few—perhaps only—scholars who have attempted to correlate faculty members' sex and ethnicity with faculty attitudes toward their work. Based on results from several faculty surveys distributed between 1975 and 1984, Cohen and Brawer (1987) assert that instructors' sex and ethnicity "do not seem to be related to the way the instructors approach their work" (p. 66). They do suggest that a faculty member's ethnicity might have "an indirect association with student transfer in the form of role modeling" (p. 66). Gender is frequently used as an independent variable in studies of community college faculty members; relevant information on gender is included as appropriate in the following chapters.

Age

Using NSOPF:99 data, Levin, Kater, and Wagoner (2006) report that in 1998 the average age of two-year college faculty members was 48.3. Their analysis included both full-time and part-time faculty members at both public and private two-year institutions. The single largest group of faculty was in the 50–54 age group (20 percent of all community college faculty). NSOPF:04 data about full- and part-time faculty members at public two-year schools indicate that their average age in 2004 was almost 50 (Rosser and Townsend, 2006). A more detailed description of age provided by the National Center for Education Statistics (NCES) (U.S. Department of Education, 2005) reported the ages of community college faculty in 2003 by age groupings. In this view, 12.3 percent were 34 or younger, 24.1 percent were 35–44, 32.4 percent were 45–54, 22 percent were 55–64, and 8.1 percent were older than 65. Although the single largest age group was 45–54 in 2003, these data suggest that the impending retirement crisis might not be as significant as some have argued—or that the worst has passed for the moment.

Teaching Area

Community college faculty teaching credit courses are typically classified as academic/transfer education faculty or career/vocational education faculty (Seidman, 1985). This distinction reflects the two major curricular missions of the community college: transfer education (which includes general education courses) and occupational-technical education, sometimes called vocational education or, more recently, career and technical education. We use the terms *vocational, occupational-technical,* and *career and technical* education interchangeably in discussing this mission and the faculty members who teach courses related to it.

Dividing faculty members into five categories, Levin, Kater, and Wagoner (2006) report that a full 47 percent of both full- and part-time community college faculty members work in academic areas, including the humanities, social sciences, and science. Another 40 percent work in the professional areas of business, computing, and nursing, occupational areas from which students frequently transfer. A much smaller percentage (8 percent) work in vocational areas such as industrial arts, drafting, and child care. Four percent work in developmental or remedial education, and 2 percent list themselves as librarians or counselors (p. 36).

Some scholars believe there is an institutional divide between career education faculty and transfer education faculty. Although the research is dated, Seidman's qualitative study (1985) of seventy-six community college faculty members in California, Massachusetts, and New York found that at least some "vocational faculty … do not feel empowered in the colleges" (p. 30). He also found "hierarchical distinctions" not only "between career and academic faculty but also within the ranks of career faculty" (p. 33). In particular, he found that women faculty teaching secretarial courses had lower status than men teaching business courses. More recently, Wolfe and Strange (2003) noted in their study of a small, rural two-year college branch campus of a university, "Success as a faculty member at Park is a function of differences in a distinctive hierarchy of disciplines, faculty preparation, and credentials, and employment status" (p. 355). Faculty in the humanities and with a terminal degree were the most likely to attain tenure, and most full-time faculty had higher status than part-time faculty, except in particular fields such as business and the technologies.

Grubb (2005) has also noted the status distinctions between career and academic faculty members. In an editorial written for the *Community College Week,* he stated, "Transferable education remains the highest-status activity on most two-year campuses and academic faculty tend to dominate faculty leadership and the administrator ranks. In a spatial reflection of status differences, the buildings for occupational programs are often located far away from the academic buildings, as if their noises, smells, and general untidiness need to be segregated from the clean, white-collar activities of academic education" (p. 4).

Although there is truth in his observation that academic and career education buildings are usually or often separate, what he does not acknowledge is that the career education buildings are often newer and better equipped than the buildings housing academic programs because of the federal and state funding available for vocational and career education programs. Be that as it may, there is also some truth in his comment about status differences. Part of the difference stems from the difference in required entry credentials. Faculty teaching transfer-level courses must have at least a master's degree, while those teaching in many vocational programs may need a baccalaureate or less. Career education faculty members are expected to have work experience in the area in which they teach, whereas individuals teaching transfer education courses are expected to have experience teaching in their subject field.

Some difference in status may also stem from career and technical education's initial placement in K–12 education, not in higher education, and from a tradition of closer connections between career and technical education faculty in both sectors. Based on their several national surveys of community college faculty, Cohen and Brawer (1987) state that career education faculty members see going to high schools to recruit students and to talk with high school teachers about the vocational curriculum as part of their jobs, whereas academic/transfer faculty members typically do not. Another reflection of status differences is that faculty members in vocational programs view teaching at a community college as greater advancement "both socially and economically" (p. 142) than do liberal arts faculty (academic/transfer faculty), according to McGrath and Spear (1991). In other words, vocational education faculty members, unlike academic/transfer faculty members, believe they gain status and improve their economic position through teaching at the community college.

Differences are also apparent between transfer education and career education faculty members in terms of teaching practices and preferred student outcomes. Based on several national surveys of community college faculty between 1975 and 1984 as well as a review of the literature, Cohen and Brawer (1987) described trends in teaching practices of transfer-level courses, according to faculty members' disciplines. They also found differences in desired student outcomes: "The humanities instructors want their students to learn to think critically ... and philosophy instructors consider most important the development of values" (p. 78). Science instructors who teach courses to science majors want their students to know and apply scientific principles. While acknowledging these disciplinary differences, Cohen and Brawer (1987) maintain that they "are not as pronounced as those found among the universities' academic departments, and they are considerably less distinct than the differences between the liberal arts instructors as a whole and the instructors in occupational programs" (p. 79).

Palmer (2002) updated this work by using data from NSOPF:99 to describe disciplinary differences among full-time faculty members. Although he found that 88 percent of faculty indicated lecture and discussion were their primary modes of instruction, it was apparent that "faculty members in vocational programs are less likely to use the lecture/discussion method as a primary class medium than are their colleagues in the liberal arts" (p. 12). Depending on their discipline, some instructors, such as those teaching in vocational programs and health sciences, were much more apt to use "labs, clinics, or problem sessions" (p. 12).

Yet another difference among community college faculty members in terms of their teaching area is whether they teach credit or noncredit courses. Those teaching noncredit courses contribute to the college continuing education mission, which strives to meet the needs of the local community, including short-term courses for business and industry. Doing so may mean offering adult basic education, corporate training, English as a second language, and leisure-time lessons such as swimming or golf. These faculty members are rarely studied, partly because most of them are part time (Grubb, Badway, and

Bell, 2003; Roueche, Roueche, and Milliron, 1995). And not all full-time faculty members are supportive of continuing education activities, as they fear these activities compete with credit offerings for institutional resources (Brewer, 1999).

Grubb, Badway, and Bell (2003) briefly discuss these faculty members in their examination of noncredit education in community colleges in four states. The noncredit programs they examined were typically staffed with part-time faculty, who, according to the authors, are treated even worse than part-time faculty teaching credit courses. The authors stress the low status of noncredit programs, saying it has been "the institution's 'stepchild'" (p. 230). Often the programs are conducted at night or off campus, so those teaching them have little or no contact with instructors teaching credit courses. In other words, faculty members who teach in noncredit programs have the lowest status of all community college faculty members, even less status than those who teach in developmental programs (Grubb, Badway, and Bell, 2003). Although Levin, Kater, and Wagoner (2006) suggest that the business and industry link through short-term courses is becoming more important in community colleges, it is not clear that this change has resulted in better treatment of faculty members who teach noncredit courses.

Those who deliver developmental courses teach noncredit courses of a different type. Unlike most noncredit courses, these courses count for college credit so their students may be eligible for financial aid. The courses rarely transfer as accepted credit to four-year schools, however. Partly because developmental courses are a kind of noncredit course and partly because developmental instructors teach students with the weakest academic background, developmental faculty members are sometimes marginalized in their institutions. Often they are physically marginalized by being placed in a developmental studies unit or program, separate from the college's other academic programs (Sheldon, 2002). Additionally, not all community college faculty support the concept of developmental education, believing it hurts the image of the community college as an institution of higher education (Kozeracki and Brooks, 2006; Sheldon, 2002). As Perin (2002) notes, "Academic discipline instructors ... view developmental teaching as a low status assignment and even a punishment" (p. 35).

Educational Credentials

As indicated earlier, the master's degree is required of those who teach transfer-level courses. In fact, it is the most common educational credential of full-time community college faculty members. In 2003, 63 percent of full-time community college faculty members teaching one or more credit courses held the master's as their highest degree, while more than 19 percent held the doctorate, 1.9 percent a professional degree, almost 12 percent the bachelor's degree, and 3.9 percent an associate's degree or equivalent (Rosser and Townsend, 2006). When part-time faculty members are included in the degree analysis, the figures change substantially. Levin, Kater, and Wagoner (2006) report that, when both groups are considered, 53.5 percent hold master's degree as the highest degree, 19.2 the bachelor's degree, and 11.8 percent the doctorate. Faculty members who teach in vocational or occupational-technical programs, including such fields as auto repair and welding, typically hold a bachelor's degree or less. A national study of the preparation and credentialing of two-year college technical instructors reported that as of 1998, seventeen states required that these instructors be credentialed by the state (Olson, Jensrud, and McCann, 2001). As part of the credentialing, ten states required a high school degree and job-related experience, two required an associate of arts degree and job experience, and five required a bachelor's degree, usually combined with limited work experience (Olson, Jensrud, and McCann, 2001). Keim (1989) found that 60 percent of all two-year college faculty (both full time and part time) were in occupational and technical areas. This high percentage helps account for the percentage of full-time community college faculty members with a bachelor's degree or less as their highest educational credential. (The topic of educational credentials is discussed in greater depth later.)

Salaries

According to Levin, Kater, and Wagoner (2006), NSOPF:99 data indicate the mean income of full-time two-year college faculty in 1998 was $53,989. Salaries varied by teaching area, with social sciences faculty earning the most ($58,504) and "low status pros" (p. 91), meaning faculty who teach in areas with low status and pay in the workforce, earning the least ($50,989). Reflecting differences in databases used, another database and definition of faculty indicate that in 2004–05 the average salary of full-time public two-year college instructional faculty on nine-month contracts was $53,932 (U.S. Department of Education, 2005). According to this same database, the average salary for a public four-year college faculty member was $66,053 ($73,913 for a faculty member in universities and $60,986 for ones at other four-year institutions. Again, the NCES (U.S. Department of Education, 2005) provides a more detailed picture of salaries. In 2003, 16 percent of full-time faculty in community colleges earned between $25,000 and $39,999. One-third (33.7 percent) earned between $40,000 and $54,999, while nearly one-fourth (23.0 percent) earned between $55,000 and $69,999. Twenty-four percent made more than $70,000 per year. This distribution of salaries was comparable to that of salaries for full-time faculty members in public comprehensive colleges.

Part-Time Faculty

As stated earlier, approximately two-thirds of community college faculty members are part time, the highest percentage in any higher education not-for-profit institutional type. In all of higher education, both the number and percentage of part-time faculty members have steadily risen over the years, but particularly so in community colleges. In 1962 part-time faculty members constituted 38 percent of community college faculty; by 1974 they were 50 percent (Palmer, 1999). In 1998, 65 percent of faculty at public two-year schools were part time (Berger, Kirshstein, and Rowe, 2001). By 2003 the percentage of part-time teaching in community colleges had risen to 67 percent (Cataldi, Fahimi, and Bradburn, 2005). Although approximately two-thirds of community college faculty members are part time, they teach only about one-third of the courses (Roueche, Roueche, and Milliron, 1995). Many teach one or two courses part time at the community college and then do not teach there again. A sizable percentage, however, is long term (Avakian, 1995). In 1992 more than 20 percent had taught ten or more years, while almost 23 percent had taught between five to nine years (Palmer, 1999).

Because part-time faculty members constitute such a high percentage of community college faculty, the reasons for their being hired need to be briefly described. The primary reason is their low cost—and thus the cost savings to the institution—compared with full-time faculty members (Lankard, 1993; Roueche, Roueche, and Milliron, 1995). Not only are they paid on a course-by-course basis but moreover few receive benefits such as medical insurance or sick leave or have the opportunity to apply for tenure (Roueche, Roueche, and Milliron, 1995; Valadez and Antony, 2001). In a national survey of community colleges' use of part-time faculty, Roueche, Roueche, and Milliron (1995) found that about a quarter of the participating institutions had a program to provide benefits; however, recipients had to teach at least three courses each term to be eligible. Thus very few part-time faculty members actually receive any benefits.

Part-time faculty members also provide staffing and curricular flexibility (Lankard, 1993). Because enrollments in particular courses and programs tend to wax and wane over time, it is cost-effective to hire part-time faculty to teach many of the heavily subscribed courses, as these faculty do not need to be retained if enrollments drop. Additionally, from an educational perspective, part-time faculty members employed in the area where they teach are valuable because they bring real-world experience to the classroom and provide contacts in the local labor market (Wallin, 2004).

Although several reasons exist to hire part-time faculty members, doing so has its downside for institutions. First, they have limited contact with students outside class and may or may not hold office hours. NSOPF:93 data indicated that less than 53 percent had any interaction with students outside class, and under 42 percent kept scheduled office hours (Palmer, 1999). Moreover, part-time faculty may be less likely to know institutional policies and programs and thus cannot advise students about them. As a result, full-time faculty may find their advising responsibilities increased as the percentage of part-time faculty increases (Palmer, 1999; Roueche, Roueche, and Milliron, 1995). Part-time faculty also do not routinely participate in other instructional activities such as choosing textbooks and other learning resources and developing course and programmatic curricula (Dickinson, 1999; Roueche, Roueche, and Milliron, 1995). Roueche, Roueche, and Milliron (1995) raise yet another concern about the use of part-time faculty. Part-time faculty are the faculty most apt to be teaching an institution's part-time students, as those students tend to take evening and weekend courses, which are most frequently assigned to part-time faculty. Equating students with at-risk students, the authors fear that "part-time faculty are being asked more often than are full-time faculty to meet one of the greatest community college challenges—instructing the at-risk student" (p. 35).

This last issue raises the key question about part-time faculty: Do students learn as much from part-time faculty as they do from full-time faculty? Levin, Kater, and Wagoner (2006) argue that the increasing use of part-time faculty members damages the quality of instruction. Little evidence exists one way or the other. Although scholars have examined possible differences between full- and part-time faculty members in instructional methods or practices (for example, Keim and Biletzky, 1999; Schuetz, 2002) and in student outcomes (see Burgess and Samuels, 1999), the studies generally find few significant differences, whatever the topic of the study. In other words, "there are limited hard data to support whether part-time faculty are any better or worse than full-time faculty" (Roueche, Roueche, and Milliron, 1995, p. 18).

A recent study using national data from the IPEDS, however, suggests the extensive use of part-time faculty has a major downside (Jacoby, 2006). Jacoby (2006) sought to examine the relationship between a public community college's graduation rates and the extent of its use of part-time faculty. Results indicated that regardless of the type of graduation measure used, "increases in the ratio of faculty … have a highly significant and negative impact upon graduation rates" (p. 1092). In other words, the higher the proportion of part-time to full-time faculty members at an institution, the lower the institution's graduation rate. The findings of Jacoby's study are already being debated, so it is likely more studies will be conducted to determine the validity of his work. Certainly at present it provides evidence for those who question the community college's growing reliance on part-time faculty.

Gender and Race or Ethnicity

Gappa and Leslie (2002) provide a recent look at community college part-time faculty using data from the 2000 Center for the Study of Community Colleges' national survey of community college faculty as well as from NSOPF:93. They conclude that "part-time [faculty] in community colleges look more like full-time faculty than is sometimes assumed. Their interests, attitudes, and motives are relatively similar" (p. 65).

So too are their demographic characteristics. Almost 50 percent of part-time faculty members in two-year colleges in 2003 were female (Cataldi, Fahimi, and Brandburn, 2005). That same year, however, the percentage of faculty of color was lower than among full-time faculty members: over 16 percent of part-time faculty members were minorities, compared with 20 percent of full-time faculty (Cataldi, Fahimi, and Bradburn, 2005).

Through the hiring of part-time faculty members, community colleges could increase the percentage of minority faculty, but it has not happened. From their national survey of community college practices regarding part-time faculty, Roueche, Roueche, and Milliron (1995) found that "affirmative action guidelines are infrequent considerations when recruiting and selecting part-time faculty" (p. 46). Twombly (2005) found the same to be true of full-time faculty members. Searches were driven by equal opportunity considerations but not by affirmative action concerns. Institutional rationales for this behavior included the difficulty in finding qualified part-time faculty members and the transient stay of most part-time faculty in the college.

Age

The available data suggest that part-time faculty members tend to be a little younger than full-time faculty. In 1993, 50 percent of part-time faculty members were 44 or younger, compared with 33 percent of full-time faculty (Palmer, 1999). In fall 2003 more than 36 percent of part-time faculty were 44 or younger, compared with almost 33 percent of full-time faculty members (U.S. Department of Education, 2005). That same year, however, almost 18 percent of part-time faculty were 60 and older, compared with almost 13 percent of full-time faculty. Full-time faculty members dominate between ages 50 and 59—more than 39 percent, compared with 30 percent of part-time faculty (U.S. Department of Education, 2005).

Educational Credentials

Part-time faculty members are most likely to hold a master's degree as their highest degree, although some hold higher or lower degrees (Valadez and

Antony, 2001). They are also more likely than full-time faculty members to hold the baccalaureate as their highest degree (Gappa and Leslie, 2002), perhaps because so many part-time faculty are in career education. For many occupational fields, it is more important that part-time faculty have real life experience in the teaching field than that they hold a particular degree.

Salaries

As might be expected, part-time faculty earn far less for teaching a course than do full-time faculty members. In 1995 Roueche, Roueche, and Milliron calculated that "the average expense to a college district for ten three-hour courses [the average yearly teaching load of a community college instructor] with new, entry-level full-time faculty is $38,225; a district could deliver the same ten courses with part-time faculty and save $21,440" (p. 35). It obviously is significantly less expensive to hire part-time than full-time faculty. NCES data from 2003 (U.S. Department of Education, 2005) show that nearly 70 percent of community college part-time faculty members reported making under $10,000 in 2003. These data do not tell us how much community colleges pay for one three-credit course.

Using NSOPF:04 data, the AAUP developed per-course pay rates for part-time faculty in terms of percentile distributions. When faculty members are paid per three-credit course, the twenty-fifth percentile amount for community college faculty is $1,397, while the ninetieth percentile is $3,000. In other words, only 10 percent of part-time faculty are paid $3,000 or more per course, while 25 percent are paid $1,397 or less per course. When faculty members are paid per credit hour, the twenty-fifth percentile amount is $49 per credit hour, the ninetieth percentile amount $909 (American Association of University Professors, 2006). Thus 25 percent of part-time faculty paid per credit hour receive less than $50 per credit hour, and only 10 percent receive more than $909 per credit hour.

Using NSOPF:99 data, Levin, Kater, and Wagoner (2006) analyzed the salaries of part-time faculty in two-year colleges by academic area, including arts and humanities, social sciences, hard sciences, computer and technology professions, trades and low-status professionals (for example, day care workers). They concluded that part-time faculty members teaching in the traditional academic areas earn more of their income from academic work compared with part-time faculty in occupational areas. For example, in the arts and humanities, part-time faculty earn 59 percent of their income from academic work, compared with 30 percent for part-time faculty in computer areas. As they note, these patterns result in significant gender differences, as women are overrepresented in teaching areas with the lowest salaries. They confirm that part-time faculty in traditional academic areas tend to earn a significant part of their income from academic work.

Palmer's analysis of NSOPF:93 data also shows differences among part-time faculty in terms of employment outside academe. More than one-third of part-time faculty members in 1992 were employed full time in positions that did not include teaching. The remaining were full-time teachers at other institutions, usually high schools (more than 15 percent), or were not employed elsewhere (more than 21 percent) or also taught part time elsewhere (almost 15 percent) or had part-time jobs not related to teaching (almost 12 percent). In other words, around 50 percent were employed full time elsewhere; the remaining part-time faculty were employed only at the community college or worked part time at the community college and elsewhere (Palmer, 1999).

Levin, Kater, and Wagoner (2006) suggest that part-time community college faculty members can be divided into two groups. The first group comprises those whose principal work and source of income is outside higher education but are hired because of their valuable expertise in specific areas. The second group comprises individuals who do not have many options outside higher education and try to make a full-time career teaching at several institutions. Institutions tend to see the latter group as cheap, flexible labor. Levin, Kater, and Wagoner (2006) suggest that vocational part-time faculty in community colleges tend to fit the first category, while part-time faculty in traditional transfer areas fit the second. In this sense a hierarchy exists among part-time faculty, just like among full-time faculty.

The rise in use of part-time faculty members has been critiqued as evidence of a "new managerial" emphasis on efficiency. Levin, Kater, and Wagoner (2006) go so far as to claim that the increasing use of part-time faculty is damaging the quality of teaching in community colleges, because part-time faculty members are usually excluded from professional development activities. By implication, part-time faculty should not be legitimized. On the other hand, these authors criticize community colleges for not providing benefits, rights, and professional development for part-time faculty. In this view, their status should be legitimized. At one point, the authors imply that community colleges have an obligation to provide careers for those who attempt to make a full-time career out of being part-time faculty.

We see these conflicting stances toward part-time faculty members as an attempt to come to terms with the phenomenon. Part-time faculty already constitute an extremely high percentage of community college faculty members, and some scholars and institutional leaders estimate this percentage will only increase as current full-time faculty retire in the next few years. Thus from one perspective, it is important to understand their issues and their needs to increase job satisfaction and commitment to the institution. Another perspective is that institutional leaders should commit their efforts to increasing the percentage of full-time faculty rather than facilitating the integration of part-time faculty in the institution. Whether and to what extent community colleges have an obligation to part-time faculty remains an interesting question. We believe, however, that part-time faculty members are here to stay and that community colleges have an obligation, in the framework of their mission, to ensure that part-time faculty have the tools to teach effectively. If they do not, the teaching mission of the community college is clearly in jeopardy. The student clientele served by the community college needs and deserves high-quality instructors, whether full time or part time.

Conclusion

As much as possible in this chapter, we have avoided comparing two-year with four-year faculty members on various demographic characteristics. We believe it is important to look at community college faculty members in and of themselves and not in comparison with other groups, particularly as the comparisons could be used to suggest limitations in the community college professoriate.

The portrait that emerges is of a faculty whose numbers are dominated by part-time members, even though the majority of courses (and number of credit hours) are taught by full-time faculty members. The community college faculty as a whole is about half female and half male, raising the distinct possibility of parity in gender relations. Many women are attracted to teaching in community colleges by the opportunity to have a balanced life. Faculty members of color, while drawn to the institution for a variety of reasons, are not represented in numbers proportionate to the percentage of minority students in community colleges. In the aggregate, two-year college faculty members are middle-aged, with a substantial percentage advancing to retirement age in the next few years. Partly because the master's degree is typically the required academic credential, a large pool of qualified applicants is available, based on credentials only, to fill the vacated positions. Those individuals who seek to teach career and technical education as opposed to academic or transfer education would also need work experience in the area they seek to teach.

Once hired, career and technical education faculty members may face a divide between themselves and those who teach transfer education. Similarly, faculty members who teach noncredit courses, including developmental education, also face status distinctions because of what they teach. Although this divide is documented through studies of community college faculty members, it is not directly addressed in literature about leading the community college. Rather it is addressed in terms of a possible curricular divide between career and transfer education and the importance of each to the community college. Institutional leaders are more attuned to issues surrounding the extensive hiring of part-time faculty regardless of teaching area and are advised to integrate part-time faculty more fully into their institutions.

Faculty Work in the Context of the Community College

TO UNDERSTAND WHAT community college faculty members do, it is first necessary to understand what community colleges do. Thus we briefly describe the community college's dominant societal mission of open access, the curricular manifestations of this mission, and the students served by the institution. We then detail role expectations for full-time and part-time faculty members. To help its faculty members meet these expectations, most community colleges provide professional development opportunities, so we examine these opportunities for both groups of faculty. The chapter concludes with a review of the literature on the job satisfaction of community college faculty members.

The Community College's Missions and Students

Typically defined as public higher education institutions whose highest degree awarded is the associate degree, community colleges have for many decades fulfilled their ascribed societal mission of providing access to higher education. They do so through an open door policy, whereby any person deemed likely to benefit from college attendance is admitted, regardless of previous academic performance and academic aptitude as demonstrated on tests.

When students seeking college credit walk through the community college's open door, they face a comprehensive offering of programs, including certificates, diplomas, and degree programs in occupational-technical and vocational or career education fields as well as the Associate of Arts (A.A.) degree program. Designed to represent the first two years of a baccalaureate degree, the A.A. is termed the academic or "transfer" degree. This degree links community colleges to higher education, as pursuing an A.A. degree has historically been community college students' first step toward enrolling in a four-year college or university. Although other degrees such as the Associate of Applied Science can lead to transfer, these degrees are usually intended to lead to immediate employment after receipt of the degree. In addition to two-year associate degrees, community colleges also have vocational certificate and diploma programs, which may take a year or less of full-time attendance to complete. Last but certainly not least, community colleges provide remedial education, community education, programs such as GED preparation, English as a second language, and short-term training for business and industry.

Thus community college faculty members teach many students who take credit courses for a variety of reasons other than preparation for transfer to a four-year school. According to a study by VanDerLinden (2002), only 21 percent of students attend community college with transfer as their only goal, although another 24 percent attend partly for future transfer but also for developing their mind and enriching their life. Career concerns are the motivation for most other students. Almost 30 percent attend to prepare for a career, while 11 percent seek to upgrade their skills so they can advance in their careers. Additionally, some students attend to take noncredit courses in developmental education or noncredit continuing education courses for their personal enrichment or career upgrading.

Faculty members at community colleges also work with students who vary in the extent to which they are committed to completing their degree. Horn and Nevill's analysis of data (2006) from the 2003–04 National Postsecondary Student Aid Study led them to create a classification of community college students in their "relative commitment to completing their respective degree programs" (p. 19). They classified students as "more committed, less committed, and not committed," depending on their enrollment status (full time or part time) during at least half of their attendance at the community college, expression of intention to transfer or complete a program, and formal enrollment in a program. Using these criteria, the authors classified 49 percent as more committed, 39 percent as less committed, and 12 percent as not committed.

In addition to offering degree programs, community colleges play an important role in economic development activities in their local communities. In this role, community colleges offer short-term training courses, most of which are not part of the college's regular credit offerings. Although this particular mission of the college is generally not the focus of most full-time faculty members, it needs to be acknowledged as an institutional function. In fact, it is this mission that Levin, Kater, and Wagoner (2006) fear is overtaking the community college's more traditional missions of transfer and career and technical education.

As a consequence of their societal mission of open access to higher education, community colleges have the most diverse student body in higher education—diverse in terms of academic ability and previous academic preparation, economic status, and demographic characteristics of sex, race and ethnicity, and age. They also tend to demonstrate behaviors such as enrollment that can work against their academic success and program completion.

Students' Academic Ability and Preparation

Community college students range in academic ability and preparation from high school dropouts to high school valedictorians. But because of their open door policy, community colleges admit a higher percentage of students with a weak educational background than do most four-year schools. This weak background is manifested in the high percentage of entering freshmen who need remedial or developmental courses. In fall 2002, 42 percent of community college entering freshmen took one or more developmental courses, compared with 20 percent at public four-year colleges (Parsad and Lewis, 2003).

Students' Economic Status

One manifestation of the institution's open door policy is efforts to make the institution financially accessible. Thus community colleges have the lowest tuition in higher education. In 2003–04 community college students on the average paid approximately $1,000 for tuition and fees (Horn and Nevill, 2006). Partly as a consequence, many low-income students enroll at community colleges. Among higher education institutions, community colleges enroll the highest percentage of students in the lowest socioeconomic quintile (Horn and Nevill, 2006).

Women and Minority Students

Low tuition, open access, proximity, and flexible scheduling may have all contributed to the extensive enrollment of women and minority students, particularly those in the lowest socioeconomic category, many of whom are nontraditional and returning students. As in all of higher education, women students have dominated enrollments for almost three decades. In 2003–04 more than 59 percent of community college students were female, according to U.S. Department of Education data (Horn and Nevill, 2006). As of 2003–04, community colleges enrolled almost half of all African American, Hispanic, and American Indian students (Horn and Nevill, 2006).

Age

Community colleges also enroll the highest percentage of older students. For several decades the average age of community college students has been higher than that of students at four-year institutions, particularly research institutions. In 2003–04, 57 percent of undergraduate students who were forty years of age or older attended community colleges (Horn and Nevill, 2006). The median age of students is dropping, however. Forty-two percent of all community college credit students were under the age of twenty-two in 2001 (Adelman, 2005), and the median age of students was 23.5, compared with 26.5 in 1991.

Enrollment Status

Community college students on average are more likely to also work than are students in four-year colleges. In 2003–04 just over 30 percent of community college students enrolled full time, compared with 63 percent of four-year college students (Horn and Nevill, 2006). Almost 80 percent of two-year college students work while attending college versus 70 percent of four-year college students. When they work, community college students are more likely to be employed full time (41 percent versus 23 percent of four-year college students who worked in 2003–04). Additionally, two-year college students worked more hours per week: thirty-two hours versus twenty-six hours for four-year college students (Horn and Nevill, 2006).

In short, community college instructors are likely to face students who differ widely in age, interests, and abilities, which in turn shapes the role of faculty in community colleges.

Role Expectations for Full-Time Faculty Members

Whether teaching community college students or students at other kinds of institutions, faculty members are expected to teach and perform other instructionally related activities such as developing curriculum and advising students. Two other roles are also traditionally associated with being a faculty member: conducting research or scholarship, and performing institutional and disciplinary service. This section examines the extent to which community college faculty participate in all three of these roles.

Teaching

Given the community college's overarching mission of providing open access to higher education, the most important role of community college faculty members is to teach, and teach they do. According to NSOPF:04 data, full-time community college faculty members teaching one or more credit courses in 2003 spent almost nineteen hours a week teaching credit classes and generated more than 438 contact hours (teaching hours multiplied by number of students). With an average work week of not quite fifty hours, including paid and unpaid institutional tasks and tasks outside the community college, the typical full-time instructor spent about 85 percent of his or her time on instruction, including advising students, grading papers, and preparing for classes (Rosser and Townsend, 2006). In contrast, full-time faculty members at comprehensive colleges and universities reported spending about 73 percent of their time on instruction, while university faculty members reported spending almost 66 percent. Teaching responsibilities were less for each of these groups as well. Those working at public comprehensive institutions spent almost twelve hours a week teaching credit classes and generated almost 318 student contact hours in these courses. At public research institutions, faculty members averaged 9.2 hours a week teaching credit classes and generated more than 320 student contact hours a week (Rosser and Townsend, 2006).

Community college faculty members are not only expected to spend most of their time on teaching, including advising students and developing curricula, but also to be committed to the success of the kind of students who attend community colleges. As mentioned, the majority of these students are nontraditional, frequently in age but also in other dimensions such as previous academic record, enrollment status, and commitments outside their education.

Research/Scholarship

Research, defined by Boyer (1990) as the "scholarship of discovery" (p. 17) and generally thought of as the creation and development of new knowledge through scholarly investigation in one's discipline, is not usually expected of community college faculty. In a 1997 national survey of community college faculty members, only 5 percent indicated that "regular research activity is expected" (Huber, 1998, Table 58) of them; thus it rarely occurs. In 1998, for example, only slightly more than 3 percent of full-time community college faculty members had published five or more publications in the previous two years and almost 70 percent had no publications at all during that time (Schuster and Finkelstein, 2006). Additionally, NSOPF:04 data indicate that the average number of articles published by community college faculty members in refereed or nonrefereed journals was less than one article in the last two years of the 2003 survey (Rosser and Townsend, 2006).

Little institutional support exists for community college faculty members wishing to do research defined in the traditional way as disciplinary scholarship resulting in new knowledge and publication. The institution rarely provides release time to do research, although some provide sabbatical leaves for completing doctoral work. Most colleges also support faculty travel to conferences to deliver papers (Murray, 2001). But other than these few activities, the culture and role expectations of community colleges may discourage faculty from engaging in traditional research. A study of faculty culture at a two-year branch campus of a university (Wolfe and Strange, 2003) stressed that working in a community college could be detrimental to conducting the level of research needed for "a progressive academic career ladder," the move "up and out" to another institutional type like a university (p. 360).

Although research as traditionally defined may not be expected of community college faculty, Boyer's groundbreaking work (1990) about the nature of scholarship provides a lens to capture the disciplinary work and study in which many community college faculty members do participate. Boyer argued that the work of the faculty needed to be considered in terms of four kinds of scholarship. The first kind is what is traditionally considered "research," the creation of new knowledge in a disciplinary area or field by conducting original research to add to the existing knowledge base. Boyer calls this kind of work the "scholarship of discovery" (p. 17). Next is the "scholarship of integration," defined as "serious, disciplined work that seeks to interpret, draw together, and bring new insight to bear on original research" (p. 19). A third kind of scholarship is applied scholarship or the "scholarship of application" (p. 21), in which the faculty member participates in "service activities … tied directly to one's special field of knowledge [that] relate to, and flow directly out of, this professional activity" (p. 22). Finally, there is the "scholarship of teaching" (p. 23), in which the faculty member takes teaching seriously, that is, maintains currency in the teaching field, plans how to teach the subject material, and "stimulate[s] active, not passive, learning and encourage[s] students to be critical, creative thinkers, with the capacity to go on learning after their college days are over" (p. 24). Some add that the scholarship of teaching involves reflecting on one's teaching and sharing the results of those reflections with others in some sort of public way (presentations or publications).

At a minimum it would appear that most if not all community college faculty members participate in the scholarship of teaching. Certainly in the last twenty years they have been called to do so. Beginning in the 1980s, Cross and Angelo (1989) stressed community college faculty members' role as classroom researchers as a way of improving how the faculty teach and what students learn.

Not only urging the scholarship of teaching, Vaughan began in the 1980s to advocate that scholarship, defined in several ways, should be an expectation of full-time community college faculty members. Although Vaughan was not the first to argue in favor of a scholarly role for these faculty (see Forbes,

1966–67; Shapiro, 1964), he has been the primary advocate. A community college president who became a university professor in a program preparing leaders for community college, Vaughan defines scholarship broadly to include the scholarship of teaching (writing textbooks and other instructional materials), assessing student learning, and original scholarship or what is traditionally considered "research." It is important to note that his definition of scholarship predates Boyer's work (1990) and clearly includes Boyer's fourth category, the scholarship of teaching. Vaughan believes that conducting scholarship is necessary for faculty members' intellectual vitality. A side benefit is increased understanding of the community college as an institutional type when its own faculty members write about it through their research on its activities (Vaughan, 1986; see also Vaughan 1988, 1992).

Vaughan is not the only advocate for the importance of scholarship for community college faculty. Palmer (1992) and Prager (2003) also believe that "scholarship matters" (Prager, 2003, p. 579) for these faculty. Palmer (1991) has been prominent among university professors who argue that the scholarship of teaching should be the focus around which community college faculty members build their professional identity.

The extent to which institutional leaders have listened to these calls for increasing scholarly expectations, at least in terms of the scholarship of teaching, is not clear, as no national study has been conducted on this topic. Some evidence suggests, however, that institutional leaders support their faculty members' efforts to maintain currency in their teaching field: at least 90 percent of institutions provide financial support for attending professional conferences (Murray, 2001).

Service

A third aspect of community college faculty members' work life is institutional service, defined as participating in faculty governance, chairing and serving on departmental and division committees, and doing some administrative tasks. In 2003 full-time community college faculty teaching one or more credit courses spent an average of just over three hours a week on administrative committees (Rosser and Townsend, 2006). Although institutional service is required, service to national, regional, or national disciplinary associations is not. Neither is it expected (although sometimes it may be welcomed), depending on the culture of a particular community college. A high percentage of community college faculty members serve as consultants or participate in professional service: 80 percent according to a 1997 national survey of their activities (Huber, 1998). This high percentage may reflect the large number of career education faculty who consult or perform service in their vocational area.

Role Expectations for Part-Time Faculty

Full-time community college faculty members perform institutional service, teach, and conduct some form of scholarship, although not necessarily research as traditionally defined as the creation of new knowledge. This description partially fits role expectations for part-time faculty members as well. In their case, however, teaching does not typically include aspects of instruction occurring outside the classroom such as curriculum development and advising. The majority of part-time faculty teach one course a quarter or semester, yet some teach almost a full load of courses (Avakian, 1995). According to NSOPF:93 data, in 1992 part-time faculty members generated almost 140 credit hours on average, compared with almost 375 hours for full-time faculty members. Part-time faculty members taught an average of forty-two students, while full-time faculty taught more than one hundred (Palmer, 1999). Occasionally part-time faculty members may be asked or may volunteer to participate in institutional service. Any participation in disciplinary organizations is strictly on their own time and typically not considered in any employment decisions by the institution. It is likely that many intuitively participate in the scholarship of teaching, defined as reflecting about what and how they teach and keeping current in their teaching field. A small percentage may also participate in original research, although there are no job expectations whatsoever that they do so.

In-Service Training and Professional Development

Given that the primary role for both part-time and full-time community college faculty members is teaching, it is important to examine whether and to what extent the community college develops teaching ability, including maintaining currency in one's field. This question is particularly important because, as indicated in the next chapter, there is currently little discussion of preparation programs and even less discussion of the skills (over and above being a good teacher) necessary for those seeking to become community college faculty. Rather, the community college has established general preparation requirements (master's degree or eighteen hours in the teaching field for transfer education faculty and typically a baccalaureate or less, plus relevant work experience, for career education faculty) and commitment to the community college mission as entry requirements. Any specific preparation for teaching at community colleges is typically done by way of in-service or professional development. For example, the search committee chairs in Twombly's study (2005) of community college job searches indicated that they relied on professional development to develop teaching skills in individuals who have potential but lack extensive teaching experience.

Faculty professional development may be so important to community colleges because the faculty who are hired may not be familiar with the "special philosophy and commitment of the community college" (Roueche, Roueche, and Milliron, 1995, p. 83), their faculty roles, or the characteristics of community college students. In particular, "there is a special need to provide induction opportunities for those who come new to the institution, especially those who come from business and industry, with no background in education" (Roueche, Roueche, and Milliron, 1995, p. 84). Given the institution's reliance on professional development, it is disturbing to find that much of the literature about professional development programs portrays them as ad hoc and uncoordinated. Grubb and Associates (1999), in their extensive study of community college teaching, go so far as to say that "most colleges have used in-service in unfocused and thoughtless ways" (p. 297).

Various terms are used for faculty development. In addition to faculty development, we found *professional development* or *in-service,* yet we could find little discussion of the differences. Cohen and Brawer (1977) suggest that development programs are concerned with the personal, cognitive, social, and affective growth of faculty as people and practitioners. They distinguish development from preparation by suggesting that the latter typically refers to "experiences structured for an individual as he develops prior to, or within, the profession" (p. 66). Cohen and Brawer acknowledge that terms referring to development of community college faculty are often used interchangeably. For them, the important thing is that development activities are intended to affect professional attitudes and abilities. From our reading of the literature, it seems that "faculty development" refers to activities directed at improving the skills needed by faculty, whereas "professional development" is a broader term that may include a broader range of institutional employees. "In-service" typically refers to a method of delivering professional development, normally through one-day workshops or other similar activities.

Components of Professional Development Programs

John Murray (1999a), the most frequently published author on the topic of professional development in community colleges, suggests that effective faculty development programs have several components: institutional support—a climate that encourages faculty development; a formal, goal-directed program; links between development and rewards; faculty ownership; support from colleagues for investments in teaching; and a belief on the part of instructors that administrators support and value good teaching. Similarly, Burnstad (1994) identifies several characteristics of effective faculty development programs: "comprehensive, supported by administration, managed by a staff developer, constituent driven, adequately funded, evaluated periodically, and supportive of the organization's mission" (pp. 389–390). We argue that some of these components, such as a goal-directed program, are characteristics of an effective program, while the remainder consist of institutional conditions that contribute to the success of the intentional, goal-directed program. Successful programs need both content and institutional support, but separating the factors identified by Murray (1999a) and Burnstad (1994) into the two categories helps draw attention to the necessary institutional support factors.

Activities

Murray has examined professional development nationally (1999a), in Texas community colleges (2000), in publicly supported two-year colleges (2001), in Ohio two-year colleges (1995), and in two-year colleges accredited by the

Southern Association of Colleges (2002). Grant and Keim (2002) also conducted a national study to assess the status of professional development for faculty. These researchers found that nearly all community colleges offer some form of faculty development. Their studies provide a picture of what community colleges offer by way of faculty or professional development.

The most frequently offered activities across all the studies are providing financial support for attending professional conferences (at least 90 percent of all colleges), bringing experts to campus to give workshops or talks (at least 88 percent), having institutional faculty provide workshops (between 69 and 93 percent), providing tuition waivers for full-time faculty at the home institution to take courses (between 67 and 77 percent), granting sabbatical leaves (43 percent in Southern Association of Colleges and Schools [SACS]–accredited colleges, compared with 63 to 69 percent at colleges in other regions and nationally), providing release time to work on projects to improve teaching (between 63 percent and 77 percent), providing a resource center for teaching effectiveness (39 percent),[1] offering some activities directed at new faculty (Murray–35 percent, SACS-accredited schools–91 percent, Grant and Keim–78 percent), and awarding minigrants for teaching improvement (between 35 percent and 61 percent of all colleges). On a whole host of other possible activities, much more variation occurred. SACS-accredited schools, for example, reimburse faculty for tuition at other colleges (66 percent) and provide opportunities to work in industry (56 percent of SACS colleges, compared with 27 percent of colleges nationally).

Institutional Support

Although the research to date shows that the vast majority of colleges have professional development for faculty members and offer a core set of professional development activities, less consensus is apparent on whether institutions support these programs. The effectiveness of professional development programs is also a matter of some debate. One measure of institutional support is the title and administrative location of individuals responsible for faculty development. Murray (2000) found that 92 percent of the individuals in charge of faculty development at publicly supported Texas two-year colleges had an administrative title and that nearly 70 percent of the positions were associated with the chief academic officer. Only 15 percent of the institutions used other administrative titles, and 15 percent had nonadministrative roles. At almost 70 percent of Texas community colleges, the chief academic officer is responsible for coordinating professional development activities. Grant and Keim (2002) found that 48 percent of the colleges in their study had no designated coordinator, 53 percent named the chief academic officer as the responsible person, and 39 percent placed responsibility in the hands of a committee.

Researchers use these data as evidence of a lack of administrative support for professional development, because the chief academic officer presumably has many other duties. A dedicated administrator would undoubtedly provide more support for professional development. What we do not know from these studies is whether the chief academic officer is merely the highest-ranking officer to whom a director reports or whether he or she actively directs faculty development activities. Murray (2001) helps clarify this puzzle, noting that 84 percent of the respondents to his study indicated spending less than 50 percent of their time on faculty development activities, while 43 percent spent less than 10 percent of their time on these activities. Part of the reason is that chief academic officers seem to have the responsibility for faculty development along with their other duties. This finding is repeated in Murray's studies of Ohio, Texas, and the SACS colleges. Further, he concludes that little evidence exists that faculty development at most colleges is anything more than a "randomly grouped collection of activities lacking intentional coordination with the mission of the college or the needs of faculty members" (2001, p. 497). These findings would seem to confirm Murray's conclusion (2001) from his national study that there is "a glaring lack of commitment to faculty development on the part of the leadership at most of the 130 community colleges" (p. 498). Although there is some indication that creation of centers for teaching excellence devoted to professional development of faculty members is on the rise, that trend is not yet reflected in the published literature.

Despite the negativity characterizing studies of faculty development activities, public community colleges tend to exhibit some characteristics of effective faculty development programs (Murray, 2001). Specifically, the vast majority of public community colleges offer a set of activities such as support for travel to professional conferences and workshops on teaching. In addition, some evidence suggests that peers and administrators alike value good teaching. The lack of leadership and absence of formalized, structured programs connecting faculty development to institutional goals, however, diminishes effectiveness of professional development efforts. Particularly noteworthy is the lack of centers for faculty development, although this situation may be changing. Murray notes that 39 percent of the public two-year colleges in his study had such centers. It is not clear from his research how professional development is related to evaluation of teaching, which does appear to be an essential component of institutional rewards. That is, no explicit link is made between participation in development activities and teaching improvement, which is then linked to evaluation.

Grubb and Associates (1999) agree with many of Murray's criticisms. Based on their qualitative study of thirty-two community colleges, they note that one of the most popular forms of staff development—the seminar or workshop by an outside expert—is less than effective because it covers a smorgasbord of topics. Faculty may or may not attend all sessions, thus failing to provide a common sense of teaching. Most serious to Grubb and Associates is that the seminars or workshops are one-shot events, doing little to build a culture of teaching and treating teaching as a simple task. As a result, faculty do not take professional development activities very seriously. In contrast, the best colleges rely more on internal resources to build a culture of teaching.

Spear, Seymour, and McGrath (1992) claim that the purpose of faculty development is to reduce the dissonance between the demands of the job and faculty's traditional training in research universities. They are critical of the fact that professional development often "single mindedly" (1992, p. 146) focuses on instruction, based on an assumption that teaching in community colleges can be divorced from disciplinary knowledge. They see faculty development as reinforcing the faculty isolation that Grubb and Associates (1999) so dramatically found in their study.

Grant and Keim (2002) conclude that faculty development has grown in breadth, depth, and scope in recent years. Further, they see faculty development as attempting to integrate professional, personal, curricular, and organizational goals. They agree with Murray, however, that the faculty development coordinator is a powerless position (if there is a position), although professional development efforts are reasonably well funded.

Burnstad (1994) also identified examples of faculty professional development programs that were comprehensive in nature and directed at supporting instructional excellence across the campus. These programs were at Johnson County Community College, Community College of Aurora, El Paso Community College in Texas, Austin Community College, and Miami-Dade Community College. She suggests that some institutions have also taken a consortium approach to professional development, but this approach is much less frequent. Various concerns emerged in her study: maintaining programs especially in light of budget cuts; preparing faculty to serve underprepared students; responding to cultural diversity; integrating technology into instruction; understanding the impact of assessment; preparing for institutional change; and training new staff developers.

Although we appreciate the criticisms of faculty development in community colleges, they seem to be based on some idealized notion of what faculty development should be rather than on an assessment of what works best, that is, what makes a difference in how faculty members perform their jobs. We suggest that, like most educational programs, there is no one best way to provide professional development. Effectiveness depends on many factors, but assessments of changes in how faculty members perform their teaching responsibilities are probably the best measures of faculty development programs.

Surprisingly, little has been written about the evaluation of these programs, although Grant and Keim (2002) note that 47 percent of programs do internal evaluations. In an evaluation of one statewide program, Sydow (2000) addresses whether participation in structured professional development results in improved teaching and learning. To address this question, she studied the outcomes of the Professional Development Initiative (PDI) in the Virginia Community College System (VCCS). The VCCS PDI includes support for discipline, instructional, career, and organizational development. Headed by a full-time director, the program "requires that each college maintain a comprehensive professional development program; encourages and supports faculty members to maintain individual development plans; and provides eight statewide, system-supported programs that contribute time, funding, and support for professional development" (p. 386). The programs include peer group conferences, research grants, teleconferences, minority faculty recruitment, leadership seminars, classified staff development, technology skills, and regional teaching excellence centers.

Although the VCCS PDI has won numerous awards, Sydow (2000) wanted empirical confirmation of the actual outcomes produced by the program. She concluded that "overall, the survey findings strongly indicated that significant long-term benefits resulted from faculty members' participation in various activities ..." (p. 390). Although the number of faculty members participating in development activities increased only slightly during the five-year period of the study, the respondents reported direct improvements in teaching for those who did participate. Faculty members found peer group conferences useful for establishing networks but also for the gains they produced through application of new techniques learned. In fact, the faculty participants tended to see peer group conferences as being more practical than other forms of professional development. The research grant component of the program had wide-ranging impact because of the vast assortment of types of grants made: for instructional improvement, teaching content–knowledge development, organizational development. The instructional projects were perceived to have direct benefits to students. In other words, these findings appear to support the effectiveness of this one particular professional development program.

Professional Development for Part-Time Faculty

Most studies of faculty development do not distinguish between programs for full-time and part-time faculty. Murray's studies (1999a, 2000, 2001, 2002) and Grant and Keim's study (2002) indicate that approximately two-thirds of colleges do something for part-time faculty but that only a relatively small percentage address them in their purpose statements for faculty development. It is not entirely clear from the national studies whether part-time faculty members are excluded from most activities. The studies do not note differences in support of travel funds; the Grant and Keim (2002) study found that 53 percent provide travel funds for both full-time and part-time faculty members.

In their national study about the use of part-time faculty in community colleges, Roueche, Roueche, and Milliron (1995) looked in detail at institutions identified by their peers as having "exceptional programs in utilizing part-time faculty" (p. 161). From among these institutions, the authors identified institutions with development programs for part-time faculty. In their book, the authors do not generalize about these programs but simply describe them. For example, the College of the Canyons in California has a three-stage associate program for part-time instructors. First is a six-hour teaching skills workshop followed by a two-day advanced teaching workshop. Participants are paid for attending the workshops. The third and final stage is a teaching analysis in which each part-time faculty member, working with a full-time faculty member, "designs an analysis that responds to his or her current concerns in the classroom" (p. 96). Once this program is completed, its participants are eligible to become an associate part-time, who earn 10 percent more than do other part-time faculty members. The program has several benefits, including providing a way for the institution to "distinguish for pay purposes between part-time faculty members who stay with the college over the long-term and those who are only there temporarily" (p. 97). More important, the program "provides a basis for improving classroom instruction while simultaneously addressing the concerns of part-time faculty members" (p. 97).

The professional development program for part-time faculty at College of the Canyons, combined with the descriptions of programs and efforts of the other eighteen selected institutions, illustrate what can be done to facilitate the teaching effectiveness of part-time faculty. What is not clear from the authors' study is the extent to which all community colleges provide at least some professional development for part-time faculty, albeit not at the level or quality illustrated by these institutions. Investing in the professional development of part-time faculty members can be an effective strategy, as part-time faculty often seek full-time positions when they become available. Unless faculty development programs involve expensive, intensive one-on-one mentoring, it would seem sensible to extend faculty development opportunities to part-time faculty members.

Job Satisfaction

Whether part time or full time, to what extent are community college faculty satisfied with their work? Does it meet their expectations of what being a faculty member is? Do they feel sufficiently supported by their institution in their efforts to perform their roles? Would they choose to stay at their institution or go elsewhere for other employment?

These questions have been answered to varying degrees in a variety of studies about the job satisfaction of community college faculty. This topic has been studied for several decades, most typically in state-level quantitative studies (see, for example, Hill, E., 1986; Hill, M., 1983; Truell, Price, and Joyner, 1998) and occasionally at the regional level (for example, McBride, Munday, and Tunnell, 1992). In the past few years researchers have begun examining the construct of job satisfaction by using national data such as NSOPF survey results.

Overall, community college faculty members are satisfied with their jobs. Using descriptive data from the Carnegie Foundation's 1997 National Survey of Faculty, Huber (1998) reported about various aspects of job satisfaction. She noted that 80 percent of two-year college faculty were satisfied with their job situation as a whole, 92 percent were satisfied or very satisfied with the courses they teach, and 85 percent were satisfied or very satisfied with relationships with colleagues. Satisfaction levels dropped when faculty responded to questions about their department and institution: 66 percent were satisfied with the management of their department and only 38 percent with that of their institution. These findings suggest that faculty are satisfied with the nature of their work but less so with the structure (department) and organization (college) where they perform this work.

Creating an overall satisfaction construct derived from a national study of community college faculty, Outcalt (2002b) found few statistically significant differences in various dimensions of satisfaction between full-time and part-time faculty. He did find that full-time faculty members were generally more satisfied than were part-time faculty members. Levin, Kater, and Wagoner (2006) reported a similar finding when they looked at job satisfaction of the two groups. Interestingly, Outcalt (2002b) reported that faculty without doctorates were slightly more satisfied than those with doctorates and that liberal arts faculty were slightly less satisfied than faculty in other fields, although in neither case was the difference statistically significant.

Sometimes subsets of community college faculty are examined for their job satisfaction. In a rare examination of job satisfaction for a specific ethnic group, Flowers (2005) used NSOPF:99 data to examine differences among

African American faculty at two-year and four-year schools. Although the data he used included both African American faculty and staff, he consistently reported the findings as being for faculty. His major finding was that "African American faculty at [two-year] institutions were more likely to report being very satisfied with their jobs than at [four-year] institutions" (pp. 323–324).

Another facet of job satisfaction that has been studied is unionized versus nonunionized community college faculty members. Finley (1991) examined ten pairs of public two-year colleges in the North Central Association of Colleges and Schools. In each pair, one college was unionized and one was not. The colleges were matched on variables such as number of full-time faculty and urban or rural setting. Using a survey of job satisfaction sent to a random sample of full-time faculty members, Finley found that union membership did not correlate with higher levels of job satisfaction on any dimension except economic (pay, benefits), and even then the difference was not significant. Nonunionized faculty members were more satisfied on the dimensions of governance, institutional support, and convenience (physical surroundings, office facilities, and workload). Finley wondered "what advantage is gained through collective bargaining with the two-year college sector?" (p. 60), given the high level of job satisfaction he found, regardless of status as a union member.

Most studies of the job satisfaction of community college faculty focus on full-time faculty members. A few recent studies, however, have examined the satisfaction of part-time faculty. Using NSOPF:93 data, Valadez and Antony (2001) used factor analysis to develop three dimensions of satisfaction: autonomy, students and demands, and rewards. The authors concluded that "faculty are satisfied with their roles but they are concerned with issues regarding salary, benefits, and long-term job security" (p. 106). In a similar study also using NSOPF:93 data, Antony and Valadez (2002) compared the job satisfaction of two-year and four-year part-time faculty and found that "those who work at two-year institutions express greater overall job satisfaction" (p. 54).

Job satisfaction is also related to turnover or intent to leave. Although turnover of faculty is a topic of import for any type of college or university, few studies have directly examined intent to leave the institution except as a factor in job satisfaction studies (see, for example, Locke, Fitzpatrick, and White, 1983; McBride, Munday, and Tunnell, 1992; Valadez and Antony, 2001). One such quantitative study did find a relationship between intent to leave and job satisfaction. McBride, Munday, and Tunnell (1992) examined propensity to leave in their study of the job satisfaction of community college faculty in the eleven states in the Southern Association of Colleges and Schools. Using stepwise multiple regression, the authors found that certain job satisfaction factors—for example, dissatisfaction with the work itself, salary, policy, and administration—were shown to influence, through direct effects only, the propensity to leave. The demographic variables of gender and highest degree held were not influential, but age was: older faculty members were less likely to leave.

The finding that older faculty are less apt to leave appears in other studies about faculty, including in Rosser and Townsend's examination (2006) of community college faculty members' intent to leave. Both full- and part-time community college faculty members were included in their national study using NSOPF:99 data. The researchers used job satisfaction as the intervening variable. Job satisfaction was defined in terms of faculty's perceptions of their decision-making authority, advising and workload, and benefits and security (Rosser and Townsend, 2006). Results indicated that older faculty members were the most satisfied. Faculty members who had previously been employed at a four-year school, particularly those who had been at doctoral-granting institutions, were not as satisfied with their current position. There were no significant differences between full- and part-time faculty in terms of job satisfaction. Regarding intent to leave, Rosser and Townsend (2006) found, just as did Valadez and Antony (2001), that part-time faculty members were more likely to leave the institution. Other demographic factors influencing intent to leave included age and years in current position. Older faculty members were less likely to intend to leave as were those who had been at their institution a long time. Whether these faculty stay because they are committed to the institution or because they "despair" (p. 139) of finding a job elsewhere is not clear. It is also possible that older faculty members intend to stay because they have ties to the community—spouses who have good jobs or children or grandchildren in the area.

In short, studies of intent to leave and job satisfaction indicate that community college faculty, whether full time or part time, are on the whole satisfied with their job. Even if they are reasonably satisfied, however, some part-time faculty would leave their current institution if they could find more stable employment elsewhere, and younger faculty, particularly those who have taught previously at a four-year college, would be more inclined to leave than would older faculty members.

Conclusion

In theory those who teach at community colleges are committed first and foremost to teaching and to enabling many students who would not traditionally be viewed as "college material" to succeed. In practice most who teach at community colleges embrace these commitments, although as Grubb and Associates (1999) argue, there may be a gap between the rhetorical commitment and the extent to which individual faculty members exert themselves to teach well and help all students. Professional development activities sponsored by individual colleges are frequent means to help faculty, especially full-time faculty members, be effective teachers. Little evidence is available to support the coherence of faculty development programs and almost none of program effectiveness. We echo the concern of Grubb and Associates (1999). Community colleges advertise themselves as teaching colleges. Teaching, not research or public service, is at the core of what they do. Teaching is the centerpiece of community college professional identity. It is somewhat disturbing, then, to find so much criticism of faculty development programs on the one hand and so little evidence that they improve teaching on the other. Although our conclusions are based on a limited range of studies, those that do focus on professional development do a good job of telling us what colleges do. It is less clear from these studies that programs are effective in helping faculty members be better teachers (that is, helping students learn better). As all colleges, four-year colleges and universities included, place greater emphasis on improved teaching and implement faculty development programs, community colleges run the risk of losing their claim to fame as true "teaching colleges." For the sake of its students, the term "teaching

Dimensions of the Community College Faculty Career

A S HOWARD LONDON (1978) NOTED IN HIS SEMINAL ethno-graphic study of the culture of a newly formed community college in Massachusetts, "To study [faculty] careers is to study identities" (p. 29). In the case of community college faculty members, a study of their careers tells us not only about the individuals who have those careers but also about the community college itself. From an organizational point of view, careers can be seen as the means through which organizations socialize, train, and reward their employees in an orderly way to accomplish the goals of the organization. From this perspective, careers consist of several components: entry points, processes that match individuals with initial entry points (searches), a series of progressively complex positions through which employees can move, and formal departure or exits from the organization. In post–World War II America, careers were seen as a way of securing, training, and motivating employees in return for a "promise" of lifetime employment.

Although faculty careers differ in important ways from the classic bureaucratic career, some commonalities exist. For instance, full-time faculty members are recruited to the organization and typically have a probationary period leading to some sort of permanent employment, which may or may not be called "tenure" in community colleges. According to classic sociological theories of careers, the promise of securing permanent employment by meeting certain criteria linked to organizational goals motivates faculty members to learn the work of the organization and do that work well (see, for example, Hughes, 1937).

Because certain aspects of the faculty career depend on the type of organization the faculty member enters—that is, different types of colleges and universities have different qualifications for faculty based on their missions—it is also important to think of faculty careers as occurring in a labor market where potential faculty members exchange their talents for rewards and colleges compete for labor. Labor markets have rules—some formal and explicit and others informal and unstated—that govern such aspects of careers as who can apply for positions, how they apply, and what the criteria are for promotion. Requirements for becoming a faculty member (entry qualifications) not only signal what skills and attributes are necessary to do the organization's work but also protect those who work in community colleges from other workers who might seek entry into the labor market (Gahn and Twombly, 2001). The extent to which community colleges hire individuals directly from graduate school or from other community colleges also indicates to what degree community college teaching has become a distinct career or profession. (We consider this topic in greater detail later.)

Much of the sociological work on faculty careers is based on a modernist notion of careers as consisting of full-time employment in one type of work—and even in one single organization—over an extended period of one's life. This version of careers, however, is no longer necessarily accurate for individuals or for organizations. This shift is particularly noticeable in community colleges, where approximately two-thirds of the faculty are now part time (Cataldi, Fahimi, and Bradburn, 2005). As a result, we include some consideration of career issues related to part-time work.

This chapter examines various dimensions of the community college faculty career, including preparation and entry requirements (academic credentials and prior employment). After looking at the search process, or how and where community colleges find faculty, it then discusses aspects of faculty members' career once in the community college: academic rank, tenure and promotion, determination of salary, and decisions to stay or leave, possibly through retiring.

Preparation to Become a Community College Faculty Member

What are the necessary qualifications or preparation to teach in a community college? Throughout the history of the community college, scholars have speculated about the answer to this question by writing about the need for specific training programs for junior and community college faculty (see, for example, Dobrovolny, 1964–65; Eells, 1936; Garrison, 1941a, 1941b; Jantzen and Cobb, 1958; Koos, 1949). In the 1930s, 1940s, and 1950s, the question of the appropriate preparation for junior college faculty was a topic of considerable importance, judging by the number of articles appearing in the *Junior College Journal,* the publication of the organization representing two-year colleges (currently called the American Association of Community Colleges). These articles considered a variety of questions. Should junior college faculty have teaching experience? Should they be required to have certificates? What, if any, professional education experiences or courses should they have? How many hours in the content area should they have? Although this literature is dated, a brief summary of some of its conclusions provides a glimpse into the origins and staying power of community college career characteristics.

Although the early literature seems to contain some debate about whether community college faculty members should be certified, it is a minor point compared with an emerging consensus on what kinds of experiences and qualifications were necessary. In part the specific issue of certification may have emerged because, as Koos (1947, 1948a, 1948b) noted, a substantial portion of junior college faculty taught simultaneously in high schools and junior colleges and thus were certified to teach in high schools.

Most authors agree that junior college faculty members needed both subject matter expertise at an advanced level as well as a considerable number of hours in education courses (Garrison, 1941a, 1941b; Koos, 1947, 1948a, 1948b; Dolan, 1952; Colvert, 1952; Eckert, 1948). A master's degree in the content area was generally agreed to be sufficient because as Garrison (1941a, 1941b) explained, "Instructors should be prepared as masters of subject matter in a course of study designed to give them a breadth of view as well as depth of insight. In such courses, research should be used as a tool for the implementation of teaching and learning" (p. 205). Although these early authors were careful to express the benefits of research for junior college teaching, they rarely proposed a doctoral degree as the preferred credential.

Perhaps most interesting is the agreement among these authors that junior college instructors should have considerable professional education coursework. They argue that ideal junior college teachers should have coursework in subjects such as psychology of adolescence, history and philosophy of education, tests and measurements, problems in higher education, the junior college, and methods of teaching (Dolan, 1952; Colvert, 1952; Eckert, 1948; Garrison, 1941a, 1941b; Jantzen and Cobb, 1958). Also interesting is the almost unanimous call for training in guidance and counseling for junior college faculty members. Although these authors rarely indicate a rationale for this requirement, we can assume that faculty members, in the absence of well-developed counseling centers, were expected to provide guidance as well as instruction to their students. Most authors also argue for previous teaching experience or practice teaching for arts and sciences faculty or, for occupational and vocational faculty, real-life experience working in the actual vocation about which they teach. Some even acknowledge that formal academic training might not be necessary for vocational faculty. It is difficult to know whether and to what extent these ideas about qualifications were a result of the close connections with high schools and emerging ideas about teacher preparation or an analysis of the "real" needs of the emerging two-year college as a postsecondary institution.

It is clear from more recent writing that the conversation about appropriate preparation of community college faculty has changed somewhat. Rarely do we hear of faculty members' being expected to have a background or knowledge of counseling and guidance, for example. Those functions have been turned over to professional staff just as they have in the four-year sector. And we no longer hear about the need for education courses such as "tests and measurement" and "philosophy of education." Neither is certification of much concern except in a few states and for career education faculty only. Today the debate (in the literature although not necessarily on two-year campuses) is less about formal preparation for teaching (specific training programs or certification) and more about what level of degree should be required. Although this debate is longstanding (going back to Russo, 1938, at least), it is prominent in the twenty-first century (Gahn and Twombly, 2001). The issue seems prompted by the increased availability of individuals with doctorates and status concerns of two-year colleges rather than by necessary qualifications to perform well (Twombly, 2005). Some authors assume that because community colleges need faculty and because there is an excess of individuals with Ph.D.s seeking faculty positions, community colleges would prefer these individuals and they community colleges. If more community colleges continue to be permitted to award baccalaureate degrees, a phenomenon we consider later, this debate will continue.

As noted earlier, in-service training or professional development has become the common way to prepare instructors as teachers. In other words, once they are hired, faculty members receive training in teaching rather than being expected to have gone through a professional preparation program before employment at the institution.

Entry Requirements

Although those seeking to become community college faculty members typically do not have to take a specific program to prepare them, they must meet certain entry requirements for specific academic credentials and prior work experience.

Required Academic Credentials

The highest degree required for entry into a faculty position is one proxy for a set of skills or knowledge believed to be necessary for the position. Research universities require the doctoral degree because it is evidence that the holder has mastered certain content knowledge as well as in-depth research skills. Moreover, the originality of the dissertation topic, a concern primarily for research universities, enables a hiring committee to judge a candidate's potential for research. Twombly's qualitative study (2005) of faculty hiring at three community colleges suggests that the master's degree in the teaching field (or eighteen graduate hours in the teaching field) is what faculty and administrators continue to define as needed to teach transfer and academic courses in community colleges while relevant work experience seems to be a primary concern for occupational faculty, who typically teach courses not accepted in transfer to four-year institutions. Surprising to those familiar with faculty hiring in four-year colleges and universities is that candidates for positions in the arts and sciences were rarely evaluated for their depth of knowledge in a field; rather, adequate knowledge was assumed if they possessed a master's degree.

Although stories abound about community colleges' preferring the doctoral degree, the available quantitative data indicate that possession of the master's continues to be the main entry qualification (Cohen and Brawer, 2003; Gahn and Twombly, 2001; Huber, 1998; Levin, Kater, and Wagoner, 2006; Outcalt, 2002b). The percentage of community college faculty reporting the master's as the highest degree has remained at around 60 percent or slightly higher for several decades. Gahn and Twombly (2001) report that 66 percent of the full-time community college faculty in the NSOPF:93 study reported the master's as the highest degree, while Outcalt (2002b), examining data from a 2000 study, reports 63 percent in this category. NSOPF:99 data reported by Diaz and Cheslock found that in 1998 62 percent held the master's degree (Levin, Kater, and Wagoner, 2006). Using NSOPF:04 data to examine full-time faculty teaching one or more credit courses in fall 2003, Rosser and Townsend (2006) found that 63 percent had a master's degree as their highest degree. The bottom line is that the percentage of community college faculty members holding the master's as the highest degree has changed very little in the last decade.

The percentage of faculty with doctorates has increased modestly over time. In the 1930s it was 5 percent; by the end of the twentieth century, it was reported as between 14 and 20 percent, depending on the database used (Gahn and Twombly, 2001; Diaz and Cheslock, 2006: Outcalt, 2002b). NSOPF:04 data indicate that slightly more than 19 percent of all full-time faculty teaching at least one credit course have a doctorate (Rosser and Townsend, 2006). As might be expected, the percentage of full-time faculty whose highest degree is the bachelor's degree has declined (Gahn and Twombly, 2001).

One reason we might expect an increase in the percentage of doctorate holders is institutions' isomorphic tendency to be more like those with the most societal prestige, that is, research universities. In the traditional concep-tualization of community colleges at the bottom of a hierarchy of higher education institutions (Jencks and Reisman, 1969), some might expect community colleges to hire faculty with doctorates when possible if for no other reason than to enhance their prestige. When community colleges list the doctoral degree as a preferred degree, they may do so for precisely these symbolic reasons. As one community college vice president stated in Twombly's study (2005) of faculty hiring practices, "If our faculty have those Ph.D.s … then we could stand up and say we are as big a boy as you are" (p. 434), or according to another dean, faculty with doctorates help community colleges get away from the high-school-with-ashtrays image that has plagued them since their founding. The drive to imitate higher status institutions to enhance prestige, however, arguably operates differently in community colleges from how it does in four-year institutions. Moreover, given their regional and local student bodies and even faculties, the competition to be the best community college in the country may be less than one finds among elite liberal arts colleges or research universities that compete nationally for the best students and faculty. Or if such competition does exist, it may serve a different function in community colleges from other sectors. Given their curricular mission of providing the first two years of a baccalaureate degree, the pressure to be more like four-year institutions is limited. If the trend toward offering baccalaureate degrees in two-year institutions continues, however, this situation will likely change.

Given what we might expect to be pressures to prefer the doctoral degree, how can we explain the preference for the master's degree? Sociologists and higher education scholars have a common explanation for it. The typical argument from the institutional point of view is that the community college's focus on the first two years of an undergraduate program and its open door admission policy necessitate breadth in content knowledge and an interest in students' success (Clark, 1987; Cohen and Brawer, 2003; Twombly, 2005). From this point of view, individuals with doctoral degrees are overspecialized, preferring research to teaching. Such specialization and research expertise are neither necessary nor consonant with the mission of community colleges.

Not all agree with this preference for what Spear, Seymour, and McGrath (1992) somewhat disparagingly call the "generic teacher" (p. 23). Community college faculty themselves, these authors have been very critical of the institution's preference for generic teachers divorced from their disciplinary roots. They argue that this preference has resulted in an atomized, journeyman professional, alienated from colleagues and disciplines. Not necessarily arguing against the master's degree as the entry qualification, they express a concern that the best teacher is being viewed in a sense as a jack of all trades and master of none.

Several caveats exist about ascertaining the educational credentials of current community college faculty. One is that studies of their degree attainment rarely report data separately for faculty in transfer programs and vocational programs. Further, some studies do not distinguish between full- and part-time faculty. Degree requirements for faculty in each of these groups may vary. Based on several national surveys of community college faculty members, Cohen and Brawer (1987, 2003) state that around 25 percent of faculty teaching transfer-level courses, faculty termed "collegiate instructors" (1987, p. 66), have the doctorate. In contrast, career education faculty rarely had graduate degrees.

Faculty seeking to teach in certain occupational-technical programs may find that only a baccalaureate or even less is required (Olson, Jensrud, and McCann, 2001), because no graduate degrees are available in their particular subject area (such as automotive repair). The current percentage of community college faculty with only a bachelor's degree is unclear. Using NSOPF:93 data, Gahn and Twombly (2001) found that the bachelor's degree was the highest degree for 10 percent of full-time faculty. Outcalt (2002b), on the basis of a national survey of community college faculty developed and administered in 2000 by the Center for the Study of Community Colleges, concluded that 6 percent of the 1,531 respondents from 322 colleges held a bachelor's degree as the highest degree. Diaz and Cheslock (2006) reported that 23 percent of community college faculty held a bachelor's as the highest degree. This analysis included both full- and part-time liberal arts and vocational faculty members, a fact that may be responsible for the higher percentage reporting the bachelor's as the highest degree. Using NSOPF:04 data, Rosser and Townsend (2006) found that among full-time faculty members teaching at least one credit course in fall 2003, almost 12 percent had the baccalaureate as their highest degree.

A second caveat relates to the timing of the receipt of the doctoral degree for those who do hold them. That is, is the doctoral degree received before entry into a faculty position or after entry? This distinction is important to understand qualifications for entry into the profession. And data to help us resolve this question are hard to find. The percentages cited above suggest that even if community faculty members hold doctoral degrees, these degrees are not by any stretch required to secure a teaching position in community colleges. It is likely that some portion of community college faculty members with doctorates earn them after working in a position for a number of years. According to Cohen and Brawer (1987), it was true for 25 percent of faculty with doctorates in 1975, while by 1983, it was 18 percent. Examining NSOPF:93 data, Gahn and Twombly (2001) reported that 27 percent of the faculty members in their study earned their highest degree (including the master's or doctorate) while employed in the current position. The majority (58 percent) earned their highest degree before assuming the current position. Gahn and Twombly (2001) argue that hiring faculty members with a bachelor's or master's degree and supporting their efforts to earn a higher degree is an efficient strategy for hiring and socializing faculty. Rather than hiring individuals with doctoral degrees whose work expectations and vision of higher education might be at odds with those of the community college, the community college gives preference to individuals with master's degrees, socializes them to the mission of the community college, and then encourages them to pursue a doctoral degree (whose cost the institution may at least partially pay for).

Yet another caveat regarding degree information for community college faculty is that, in contrast with four-year colleges and universities where the terminal degree is almost always in the teaching field, community college faculty members may have terminal degrees in fields other than teaching. In fact, the master's or doctorate may be in a field such as education as long as the candidate or faculty member has at least eighteen graduate hours in the teaching field. Although we found no studies reporting type and subject of degrees for community college faculty, we assume that faculty in all teaching areas are more likely to earn a terminal degree in education than are four-year college faculty.

Prior Employment

Besides having the requisite academic credentials, how else do individuals prepare for a career as a community college faculty member? One way of determining other important aspects of preparation for community college faculty positions is to look at where faculty come from and what types of previous work experience they have. Do they come directly out of graduate school, from secondary schools, or from other sources? The answers to these questions not only give us a glimpse into what community colleges value in their faculty but also tell us something about the community college as an organization and about the profession of community college teaching—and whether and to what extent community college teaching is a career unto itself.

Until at least the 1960s, it was common for community and junior college teachers to have experience teaching in high schools or elementary schools (Cohen and Brawer, 2003). Partial evidence for this statement is a flurry of 1940s *Junior College Journal* articles about the preparation of junior college teachers. In a 1941 publication, Garrison (1941a) concluded from his survey of two-year college faculty members that 70 percent had teaching experience in high schools, 35 percent in colleges and universities, and 38 percent in elementary and junior high schools (p. 138). Garrison also asked two-year college leaders which type of experience they preferred their faculty to have. Their first preference was previous experience in another two-year college followed by college or university teaching and then high school experience. Garrison (1941b) noted, however, that a substantial number of respondents rated both college and university and high school experience first. Previous teaching experience of some sort was a nearly unanimous requirement.

Garrison's study shows us that even in the 1940s the debate about the identity of the then-named junior college was raging. Was it an extension of secondary education or was it part of higher education? The answer affected the desired work experience. Garrison noted that no available evidence informed leaders as to whether high school or college teaching was a more efficacious background for junior college teachers and that most pronouncements on the subject were a matter of opinion as to whether the college was a college or an extension of high school. In the late 1930s, a number of prominent educators preferred to think of the junior college as a distinct entity separate from high schools, although it appears that freestanding, independent junior colleges were in the minority at the time (Koos, 1947, 1948a, 1948b).

In 1947 and 1948, Leonard Koos published the results of an extensive study of junior college faculty members. In this study, he identified three types of junior colleges: freestanding two-year colleges, junior colleges associated with high schools, and junior colleges associated with four-year schools. Koos (1948b) reported that only 30 percent of academic instructors in stand-alone junior colleges lacked high school teaching experience. He concluded that the "great majority of all teachers in all three types of colleges—and, therefore, in all the junior colleges represented in the investigation—had backgrounds of high school teaching experience" (1984a, p. 464). In fact, the majority of faculty in Koos's study taught in associated colleges or simultaneously in high school and junior college. When he looked at the last previous position of the instructors in his sample, he found that 62 percent came to their job from a high school teaching position (or in some cases were teaching concurrently in the high school and junior college), 7.3 percent came from another two-year college, 12.7 percent from another college or university, 12 percent from another educational position, and only 6.2 percent had no previous work experience (1948, p. 467). These findings and findings from other studies (Dolan, 1952; Garrison, 1941a) generally suggest that junior colleges were an integral part of high schools. Thus the trend of junior college teachers coming from high school was deemed appropriate until a more appropriate source could be determined or found.

In the last half of the twentieth century, the trend of hiring junior and community college faculty members directly from secondary or elementary education dropped dramatically. Cohen and Brawer (2003) reported a high percentage (64 percent) with high school teaching backgrounds in the 1950s but a drop to 44 percent by 1960. Looking at NSOPF:93 data, Gahn and Twombly (2001) reported that 15 percent of full-time community college faculty members had worked in an elementary or secondary school immediately before assuming their community college faculty position. About the same percentage came from a college or university, while 32 percent had previously been in a community or junior college. Another third had held some sort of job in a noneducational setting such as consulting (5 percent), hospital/health care (9 percent), business (12 percent), the federal government (5 percent), and the nonprofit sector (2 percent) (p. 270).

What we do not know from Gahn and Twombly's study (2001) is whether individuals who were community college faculty members in 1993 had ever taught in elementary or secondary schools. Concentrating on the immediate prior position to the current position at the community college, Gahn and Twombly (2001) did not examine whether faculty members in their study had taught in elementary or secondary schools at some earlier point in their careers. Undoubtedly the percentage with previous but not immediate experience in that setting would raise the 15 percent somewhat but not to the 60 percent levels found up to the 1960s. Nor is it possible to tell with any great certainty from Gahn and Twombly's study what percentage of community college faculty members in the NSOPF:93 study came directly from graduate school. The authors did note that approximately 170 (15 percent) of the 1,077 full-time faculty who reported no previous positions earned their highest degree the same year they took the community college teaching position, suggesting that a relatively small percentage of new faculty members are hired directly from graduate school.

Some important differences exist in sources of community college faculty members by academic area. For example, faculty members in the NSOPF:93 study (Gahn and Twombly, 2001) in areas associated with general education or the transfer mission (humanities, social sciences, and sciences) were most likely to have held an immediate previous position in another two-year college, followed by four-year colleges, and then elementary or secondary schools. Among humanities and social science faculty, 27 percent came to the community college from a four-year institution. In contrast, over half the science faculty had held an immediate previous position in a two-year college, while 20 percent had held a teaching position in an elementary or secondary school and 18 percent had held positions in four-year colleges or universities. Occupational and business faculty were most likely to have held immediate previous positions in other two-year colleges (29 percent occupational, 34 percent business), business (26 percent occupational, 25 percent business), and elementary or secondary schools (12 percent occupational, 15 percent business). Faculty members in health care areas were most likely to have held their immediate previous position in the health care industry (51 percent), compared with 24 percent in another two-year college and 11 percent in a four-year college or university (Gahn and Twombly, 2001).

In sum, the preferred entering educational credential for community college faculty members is currently the master's degree, with a minimum of eighteen hours in the teaching field. Individuals wishing to teach in some occupational-technical programs need only a baccalaureate degree at best, sometimes an associate degree, or even a high school degree, because more advanced academic credentials in their particular subject area are not available or not deemed necessary for what they teach. Desired work experience before teaching at the community college typically includes teaching at other institutions, which may be high schools, other two-year colleges, or four-year colleges. Those seeking a position teaching vocationally oriented programs are very apt and may even be required to have work experience in related occupations such as health care institutions, business, and industry.

These trends can be viewed several ways. One is that community colleges are not distinct labor markets. They have lower entry requirements (master's degree compared with doctoral degree, for example) and hire individuals from sources other than graduate school or other community colleges. On the other hand, the labor market characteristics can be viewed as maximizing all sources of talent to serve a wide-ranging mission and student body. As institutions located between high schools and four-year institutions or between high schools and the work place, one might expect community colleges to draw on sources on either side to procure talent.

Other Possible Requirements

Although one might think that given its mission, the community college would require demonstrated expertise in teaching (as opposed to merely having held teaching positions) as an entering qualification, the evidence suggests otherwise. Flannigan, Jones, and Moore (2004) point to a strong emphasis on credentials and scholarly development as opposed to teaching ability, an emphasis they do not believe suits the community college well but one that has changed little over time. From our review of literature from the first half of the twentieth century, we would argue that community colleges in their formative years were concerned about the preparation of faculty members as teachers. Recent studies by Grubb and Associates (1999) and Twombly (2005) raise similar questions about preference for credentials (degrees or working experience) and lack of attention to demonstrated teaching ability. Grubb and Associates (1999) note that "quality of teaching seems to sink to the bottom of the list" of qualities emphasized in the hiring process (p. 286). Both Grubb and Associates (1999) and Twombly (2005) confirm that community colleges judge teaching potential largely on the basis of a fifteen- to twenty-minute teaching demonstration, not an extensive evaluation of a candidate's teaching performance. On the other hand, it is clear from Twombly's study of searches (2005) that community college hiring committees and deans claim that teaching ability and concern for students are the primary criteria they apply in looking for new faculty members.

The Search Process

If demonstrated teaching ability is not a primary criterion for choosing faculty, what criteria are important? The search is the process by which candidates are matched with jobs and thus is a key link in the faculty labor market. By focusing on the search process, we learn what institutions value through the criteria they set for their primary workers—in this case faculty members—and the way in which they apply them to individual candidates. We also learn much about the labor market: where colleges have to advertise to get faculty members and where faculty members come from. The underlying theme in the literature on faculty searches is that if community colleges understand the recruitment and interview process better, they will be able to recruit more applicants and make better choices.

Although scholars of community colleges have long studied community college faculty's prior work experience and highest degree held, other aspects of the faculty labor market have garnered less attention, such as how and where community colleges find faculty and the search process through which they do so. Recently, perhaps haunted by the specter of a wave of retirements (and thus a concomitant demand for new hires), several scholars have focused on the search as the key process through which community college faculty are recruited and selected.

One thing is clear from the scant literature on this topic: the search process for full-time faculty has become more formal over time (Flannigan, Jones, and

Moore, 2004; Rafes and Warren, 2001; Twombly, 2005). Using a variety of anecdotal and archival sources, Flannigan, Jones, and Moore (2004) provide a historical perspective on the search and hiring process. Until the last twenty years or so, the process was described as very informal and following few procedures. "Handshake" and "random" are words used to describe the process. Perhaps as a result, faculty hired in the 1960s "did not bring to their faculty positions a wealth of college teaching or research, but instead obtained positions with minimum requirements, gaining knowledge on the job" (Flannigan, Jones, and Moore, 2004, p. 829). It would no longer appear to be the case. Current search processes now follow the equal opportunity guidelines described by Rafes and Warren (2001) and are far more systematic than in the 1960s and 1970s.

Steps in the current hiring process include writing a position description and advertising the position, screening candidates by a selection committee, interviewing candidates (including candidates making a teaching demonstration), and deciding whether or not to offer the position.

Recruitment

Community colleges recruit faculty by posting position announcements internally for a short time and then externally. We know little about the recruitment process. Twombly's study (2005) of searches suggests that colleges assess the strength of available talent in deciding whether to advertise internally, regionally, or nationally. Most advertise regionally and nationally through a mailing list server and in venues such as *Chronicle of Higher Education.* Winter (1996) and Winter and Kjorlien (2000a, 2000b) conducted a series of experimental studies about recruiting community college business faculty members by asking master's students in M.B.A. programs to rate the attractiveness of job announcements. Winter (1996) found that among a pool of M.B.A. students seeking faculty positions in community colleges, jobs in compensatory or developmental education programs were viewed less favorably than jobs in occupational programs, which were viewed less favorably than positions in academic transfer programs. Winter and Kjorlien (2000a, 2000b) found that jobs that did not require relocation were more favorably received. Additionally, jobs presented by recruiters with similar backgrounds (business) were viewed more favorably than jobs presented by recruiters from other areas. One conclusion from these studies is that recruiting business faculty is often a local task and that potential faculty members are often entrenched in the community. In the case of recruiting business faculty, it seems that recruiting strategies do matter. The Winter (1996) and Winter and Kjorlien (2000a, 2000b, 2001) studies suggest that certain steps can be taken to enhance recruiting efforts.

Twombly's study (2005) of community college searches for full-time faculty members in arts and sciences supports the finding of regionalism. Although the three colleges in her study advertised nationally as well as regionally, they usually hired regionally. Even if candidates were not currently living in the college's region, they often had ties to the region. In fact colleges *and* candidates seemed to prefer this outcome. They often viewed candidates from either coast with more than a little suspicion. Additionally, her unpublished data about vocational and occupational searches in these colleges indicate that these searches almost always look locally for faculty. Current full-time career and technical education instructors often had previously taught at the institution part time or had known people at the college. One factor driving the local or regional focus of searches is that community colleges may reimburse the successful candidate only for travel expenses (Twombly, 2005). Geographic location of the college certainly plays a role in recruitment. It is likely much easier to find a ready pool of faculty candidates with master's degrees in urban than rural areas. Likewise, recruitment efforts probably vary by discipline. It is much more difficult to find science and math faculty than English or social science faculty.

It is not clear to what extent serving as a part-time faculty member is a stepping stone to a full-time position. Grubb and Associates (1999) suggest that it is, while Twombly (2005) is more hesitant in her conclusions regarding the part-time advantage.

Recruiting potential faculty members is an important issue for community colleges because, as Fugate and Amey (2000) argue, some of those who become community college faculty have not always seen teaching there as a desired career goal. In their qualitative single-institution study of faculty members in their few years at the community college, Fugate and Amey (2000) found that faculty who chose to teach at Midwest Community College did so because they did not want to go through the tenure process, which was viewed as a deterrent to teaching in a four-year institution. Most wanted to teach and some did not have a doctoral degree, limiting their institutional options. Wolf-Wendel, Ward, and Twombly (2007) and Twombly (2005) have also noted that community college teaching at some point becomes an attractive option for many faculty members. That is, many individuals who take positions in community colleges choose to do so because they want to teach there as opposed to ending up there because they failed as faculty members at four-year colleges. Additionally, for those with the master's as the highest degree, the community college may be a more attractive choice than high school teaching. The point is that community colleges need to actively recruit faculty, and part of that effort is encouraging potential faculty members to consider teaching in a community college.

Nature of Interview

Searches, including interviewing and selecting candidates, are carried out by faculty committees. Flannigan, Jones, and Moore (2004) and Grubb and Associates (1999) are very critical about the interview process as the means of selecting faculty. They criticize the use of ad hoc committees whose members are not trained, whose questions are not consistent, and who function with ill-defined criteria for selecting the best candidate. Murray (1999b) and Rafes and Warren (2001) have attempted to provide guidelines for overcoming some of these barriers. In most community colleges currently, the faculty search process follows the formal "best practices" guideline set forth by Rafes and Warren (2001).

The assumption underlying these criticisms is that using faculty committees and interviewing to select instructors somehow results in poorer or less-qualified faculty than some more formally consistent process. It may be somewhat unfair and misplaced to criticize the interview process. Rather, the task of selecting faculty is itself a challenging one primarily because the work of faculty members is not routine in the same way that factory work is. Success in the job is contingent on many factors, including the relationship established by an individual faculty member and a specific class in a specific semester. The focus of the interview, in the case of community college faculty searches, is to determine the best teacher who fits best with a particular college. In part the task in community college faculty searches is made both easier and more difficult by the college's emphasis on teaching. Candidates' attributes such as status of degree-granting institution, reputation of graduate advisor, topic of thesis, and knowledge of subject matter (attributes that can be judged by their place on a hierarchy) are not particularly important (Twombly, 2005). Likewise, searches often yield multiple candidates who have relatively equal qualifications; because easily judged characteristics such as status of degree-granting institution are not important, one is left to judge based on potential. What is surprising is the relatively little time spent during the interview process on a candidate's teaching ability. Search committee participants in Twombly's study (2005) believed they could determine, on the basis of a fifteen-minute teaching demonstration to the search committee, who would be a good teacher. When they were in doubt about a candidate, the attitude was that their strong faculty development offices could assist any faculty with teaching problems.

Bases for Hiring Decisions

Knowledge of community colleges seems to be a prerequisite for the successful candidate though often not a formal requirement. The three colleges in Twombly's study (2005) of searches were concerned about fit with the community college mission, teaching potential, and fit with the college and community. In addition, Grubb and Associates (1999) cited "familiarity with community colleges and allegiance to its sacred norms [open access, student centeredness]" as important criteria for hiring in many colleges (p. 288). Attributes such as status of the institution from which the highest degree was earned or reputation of the graduate advisor do not seem to be at all important in community college searches (Twombly, 2005).

Career Stages

Little scholarly attention has been paid to the stages of a community college faculty career. When speaking of community college faculty, we tend to think of two stages: the probationary period and permanent status. Once faculty are granted tenure or pass the probationary stage, discussion of stages ceases. Faculty are assumed to be at the same point and have similar needs regardless of whether a rank system exists or not. Fugate and Amey (2000) attempted to fill part of this gap in knowledge by studying stages in the early career (first six years) of community college faculty at one Midwestern community college. In particular, they were interested in whether the role changed after a faculty member earned permanent status. In summary, "Community college faculty in this study conceptualized their role primarily as teacher. Teaching involved going beyond the subject matter to facilitating learning itself and preparing students for their careers. Supplemental components of service to the community, service to the institution, and research were part of most faculty member's role definitions" (p. 6). What little change in role there was seemed to appear between the first and second years, when faculty members began to approach teaching differently and to take on supplemental roles. Teaching was facilitated by institutional professional development, which beginning faculty members found essential to their success. Fugate and Amey concluded that instructors at Midwest Community College did not view the probationary period (three years) as a distinct and dreaded stage as do many four-year college and university faculty when they think about the tenure track. There may be some indications that this situation is changing and that the pretenure period is stressful for faculty in community colleges as well (see, for example, Wolf-Wendel, Ward, and Twombly, 2007). If it is, it represents a significant change in what is believed about faculty careers in community colleges and bears further study.

Academic Rank

Not all community colleges use ranking systems for their faculties. Rhoades's study (1998) of union contracts found that only 25 percent of the two-year college contracts had rank structures built into their salary scales. Some schools use only the title or rank "instructor"; hence, there is no advancement in rank. In a national study conducted in 1997, 9 percent of the full- and part-time faculty respondents indicated they did not have a designated rank. Of those who did, 38 percent had the title instructor or lecturer, 9 percent the title assistant professor, 13 percent the title associate professor, and 25 percent the title professor (Huber, 1998).

Today more community colleges may have academic titles, but it was not until the 1960s that many community colleges began to have a system of academic ranks (Blocker and Wolfe, 1964–65; Tillery, 1963). In 1962 less than 20 percent of public two-year schools had ranks; by 1964 it was 32 percent (Blocker and Wolfe, 1964–65). The current percentage is unknown. Reasons for adopting academic ranks included emulating universities, improving faculty, and increasing two-year colleges' status (Blocker and Wolfe, 1964–65). In the classical view of organizational careers, ranks are a way to motivate and reward faculty for work contributing to the organizational mission. Not having ranks linked the institution to secondary education, while having ranks seemed to make its faculty part of higher education.

Initial designation of rank depends on previous work experience, usually number of years taught, and entering educational credentials. The level of required credentials varies, depending on one's teaching field and nature of courses taught. Faculty who teach transfer-level courses are typically required to have a master's degree with a minimum of eighteen hours in the teaching field, while faculty who teach occupational and technical courses may need only a bachelor's degree or less (because graduate degrees are not available in their teaching field). As indicated previously, some states require only a high school or A.A. degree plus several years of relevant work experience for instructors of technical subjects (Olson, Jensrud, and McCann, 2001).

Promotion to a higher rank depends at a minimum on time in previous rank, educational credentials, and teaching performance. In some states faculty members teaching transfer-level courses typically need a doctorate to advance to full professor, while faculty teaching occupational-technical courses typically need a master's degree (in the Virginia Community College System, for example). The ease or difficulty in achieving a promotion in rank is not clear, as almost nothing has been written about this topic. One commentator stated, "Ranks … are typically determined automatically through years of service rather than through achievements in teaching or in the discipline" (Kelly, 1990, p. 2).

Tenure and Promotion

As with academic ranks, little has been written about the tenure and promotion process in community colleges. NSOPF:04 data suggest that the majority of people hired to be full-time community college faculty members seem to start on a tenure track. Over 74 percent of the public two-year college respondents indicated there was a tenure system at their institution. Almost 50 percent of the respondents were tenured, over 15 percent were on the tenure track, and just over 10 percent were not on a tenure track (Cataldi, Fahimi, and Bradburn, 2005). Data from the 2005 IPEDS fall staff survey reveal a similar picture. Almost 42 percent of the full-time faculty members were tenured, and almost 15 percent were on the tenure track. Thus 43 percent were nontenured and not on the tenure track (Keller, 2006).

Rarely do part-time faculty members have the opportunity to receive tenure. NSOPF:04 data indicate that of the part-time community college respondents, almost 83 percent were not on a tenure-track; moreover, almost 13 percent were at an institution without tenure. Thus under 5 percent were tenured or on a tenure track (Cataldi, Fahimi, and Bradburn, 2005).

Full-time faculty members not on a tenure track may have contracts subject to renewal each year or may have term contracts of three to five years in length, also subject to renewal at the end of the term. In 2001 the West Virginia Higher Education Policy Commission considered the creation of a new faculty category, term faculty, for faculty at community and technical colleges. This category would provide greater job security for faculty members than the traditional one-year contract given to faculty who were not tenured or on the tenure track (West Virginia Higher Education Policy Commission, 2001). How typical the use of full-time faculty term contracts is in community colleges with a tenure system is not clear because so little has been written about hiring and tenure at community colleges.

The typical probationary period ranges from three to seven years. According to Cohen and Brawer (2003), the normal tenure period was three years; faculty in Fugate and Amey's study (2000) also had a three-year probationary period. In California the probationary period is now four years (Collins, 2002). A report by a consultant to the West Virginia Higher Education Policy Commission indicated that several community colleges have a seven-year tenure period (West Virginia Higher Education Policy Commission, 2001).

Little is known about the criteria or process of earning tenure or permanent status in community colleges. When candidates go up for "permanent" retention, which may be tenure in some institutions, or when they apply to be promoted, they prepare a dossier or portfolio of evidence to support their case. According to a study conducted by Murray (2000), in the Texas community colleges with tenure systems, information considered important in granting tenure to faculty includes student evaluations of their teaching and administrative and peer evaluations. Similarly, his national survey of individuals responsible for faculty development in community colleges found student evaluations, administrative evaluations, and peer evaluations to be important in promotion decisions. Administrative evaluations were the most important, followed by student evaluations and then peer evaluations (Murray, 2001). Peer evaluations for both promotion and tenure are those of internal peers, not peers in other community colleges or other types of higher education institutions.

According to Redmon (1999), Central Oregon Community College's process includes a designated evaluator and a peer team to work with the person seeking promotion or tenure. The process also includes classroom visits to observe the individual's teaching and evaluation of materials the instructor provides to students.

According to one author, "Tenure is generally granted almost automatically, with just a few evaluations of teaching and usually no evaluations of scholarly involvement" (Kelly, 1990, p. 2). The accuracy of this statement is unclear, although Grubb and Associates (1999) found that "almost universally" faculty claimed that "the process for evaluating and promoting faculty members is 'not meaningful' or 'just a rubber stamp'" (p. 290). The faculty also indicated that "almost no one is denied tenure" (p. 290), so once hired and on a tenure track, a person is "likely to be given tenure" (p. 293).

It appears from Murray's various studies of faculty development that administrators play the most significant role in evaluating faculty members for promotion where a rank system exists or for tenure and merit pay. Peers and student evaluations seem to play less of a role in these institutional reward systems. Thus it is not entirely clear to what extent and how professional development and effective teaching are linked directly to institutional rewards such as tenure or promotion, although Murray's work suggests that some attempt has been made to do so. The results of participating in professional development activities could of course result in better administrative reviews. It is also unclear from Murray's studies what individuals are considered administration. Certainly at four-year colleges and universities, department chairs play a key role in promotion, tenure, and merit pay, although peer evaluation (in many cases external peers) may play a more significant role in the four-year sector.

Determination of Salaries

Unlike most four-year colleges and universities, the salaries of the majority of community college faculty members are guided by fixed salary schedules. Two-thirds of unionized community colleges have such salary schedules (Rhoades, 1998). In these cases, yearly annual increases may be determined by steps on the scale or negotiated across-the-board raises. A person's beginning salary or placement on the schedule may be determined by factors such as seniority, degrees, course credits, and previous relevant experiences (Grubb and Associates, 1999; Rhoades, 1998; Twombly, 2005). Rhoades concluded that degrees and course credits were the most common factors in determining initial placement on the salary schedule as well as for salary adjustments (Rhoades, 1998). He calls them "proxies for merit" and notes that when merit provisions are included in community college contracts, they are often designed to make salaries among faculty more equitable rather than achieve differences based on qualifications or outstanding performance.

Some community colleges have merit pay, but the percentage is unknown. According to Grubb and Associates (1999), Colorado has merit pay for faculty, regardless of institutional type. Less than 20 percent of the respondents to Murray's national study of professional development (2001) said their institution has a merit pay system. Like tenure and promotion decisions, student evaluations and administrative and peer evaluations are important factors in merit pay decisions, with administrative evaluations the most important (Murray, 2001). A study about the use of faculty evaluations in Texas community colleges (Campion, Mason, and Erdman, 2000) found that almost 17 percent of the respondents said student evaluations of faculty were "significant" (p. 176) in determining pay increases. Two of the thirty-two institutions examined by Grubb and Associates (1999) considered publications as a factor in pay increases, which the authors claim is "precisely the wrong policy for an institution that aims to be a teaching college" (p. 293).

A number of factors figure into community college faculty salaries. Less driven by a national market for faculty and more regional in their focus, community colleges with local funding are constrained by the wealth of their districts when setting salary schedules. It appears that community colleges do compare peers' salaries when setting or adjusting salary schedules, but it is not clear to what extent. The three colleges in Twombly's study of the hiring process (2005) compared their salaries with those in similar community college districts in the region, and even with those of local public school districts, but it is not known how widespread this practice is.

Community colleges do not typically adjust salaries for teaching field, at least at unionized institutions, according to Rhoades (1998). In his study of union contracts, he notes that adjustment provisions based on the market (differences for different fields of study) are not widespread in community college collective bargaining agreements. (This situation may be changing, but again such a change has not been documented in the published literature.) In contrast to this perspective, Levin, Kater, and Wagoner (2006) report salary differences by teaching field, an interesting finding given the tendency of salaries to be driven by salary schedules. They report that average salaries of full-time faculty members in the social sciences were the highest ($58,504) followed by faculty in professional areas such as business and health professions ($55,587), computer technology ($55,521), trades ($54,408), hard sciences ($54,401), arts and humanities ($52,168), and low-status professions ($50,989). If Rhoades (1998) is correct that merit and market do not make as much a difference in community colleges, we can interpret these results as being indicative of age, seniority, and differences in highest degree held.

Although community college faculty salaries are the lowest in academe, there is often little difference between the salaries of two-year and comprehensive colleges (U.S. Department of Education, 2005). The most extreme differences are between two-year colleges and research universities (ERIC Clearinghouse for Community Colleges, 1994). NSOPF:04 data show only a $5,300 difference between the total income of full-time faculty members at public associate's colleges and those at public master's institutions, with the basic institutional salary of the two-year college faculty $4,700 less. In contrast the basic salary of faculty at public doctoral institutions was almost

$28,000 more than that of two-year college faculty members (Cataldi, Fahimi, and Bradburn, 2005). Salaries among the states are also vastly different. Iowa and North Carolina have the lowest community college salaries in the nation (ERIC Clearinghouse of Community Colleges, 1994; Iowa State Education Association, 2005). Unionization of faculty may be a factor in some states. Those that permit unionization of community colleges also appear to have higher community college salaries than those states prohibiting unionization of public employees. Cohen and Brawer (2003) indicate, however, that higher salaries are a result of these states' having higher wages generally than a result of unionization.

An earnings gap also exists between female and male faculty at all institutional types, although the gap is the least at community colleges, particularly those without faculty ranks. According to an AAUP national study of faculty salaries, "Women earn on average 96 percent of what men earn at community colleges without rank; 93 percent at community colleges with rank" (Curtis, 2004, p. 2). In other words, community colleges appear to be the most gender-equitable institutions in salary determinations (see also Perna, 2003).

Faculty Retention

Given the current context of massive impending community college faculty retirements, declining pools of applicants (Twombly, 2005), and the fact that rarely is teaching in the community college a career destination, it seems essential to retain current community college faculty members. A few recent studies have examined factors affecting the intent of community college faculty members to leave or to stay at their institutions. In a study at one institution of the relationship between faculty perceptions of organizational structure and turnover intent, Dee (2004) found that turnover intent was low to moderate, with younger faculty members being more intent to leave than their older colleagues. The only set of factors significantly predicting turnover intent was "support for innovation—the extent to which an organization supports change-related activity among its members" (p. 596). When faculty members perceived innovation as well supported, they were less likely to intend to leave. Dee suggests that colleges' change activities should be designed in ways to enhance commitment to the institution.

A national study of the intent of community college faculty members to leave relied on NSOPF:99 data to examine the influence of selected demographic variables, quality of work life, and job satisfaction on intent to leave (Rosser and Townsend, 2006). The authors developed an empirical model to illustrate the interplay among faculty work life, job satisfaction, and intent to leave. Faculty work life comprised three dimensions: administrative support and facilities, professional development, and technology support. Perceptions of job satisfaction were based on ten variables that reflected the dimensions of decision-making authority, advising and workload, and benefits and security. The analysis revealed that "the observed variables [making up] the latent construction (an abstract concept that cannot be observed directly in data but are related to observed variable) of [work life] contributed significantly in the definition and measurement of faculty members' quality of [work life] ..., their satisfaction ..., and their intent to leave ..." (p. 136). The demographic characteristics of age, years in current position, prior employment at four-year institutions, and full-time versus part-time status were related to job satisfaction and perceptions of work life and intent to leave. Faculty members who had been at their institution for a long time were less positive about their work life but were less likely to leave than those who had been there for a shorter time. Not surprisingly, part-time faculty were more likely than full-time faculty members to leave for another position. The authors did not offer suggestions as to what administrators could do to retain faculty members.

It appears from these two studies that increased technological and administrative support and support for innovation would enhance faculty perceptions of their work life and thus contribute to their retention. For reasons mentioned above, retention of community college faculty members is an issue deserving much more scholarly attention.

Retirement

Some faculty members leave their institution by retiring. Although studies of intent tap some of the reasons faculty members choose to retire, they typically do not examine stages of the retirement process. By contrast, Harris and Prentice (2004) examined the stages individual community college faculty go through in deciding to end their academic careers and leave the cultures they helped to build. Using Ebaugh's Role Exit Theory to frame their study and its results, the researchers noted that in Stage One employees begin to experience doubts about continued employment. The community college faculty members in their study noted exhaustion, burnout, dissatisfaction with organizational changes as "push" factors (factors leading them to retire), and financial incentives as a "pull" factors (incentives to retire). ("Push" and "pull" are our terms, not those of Harris and Prentice.) Personal reasons could be either push or pull factors. Actions taken during this stage to alleviate the burnout and dissatisfaction included taking classes to learn new technologies, maintaining work, disengaging by "letting up" (p. 734), and participating in celebratory activities.

In Stage Two, faculty members began to seek alternatives to their current employment, including teaching part time and working in the occupation from which they had come. Most were interested in pursuing hobbies and traveling. Some had no fears but others were concerned about finances, loss of identity, and loss of work-related relationships. To accomplish their goals, faculty began pursuing their post retirement plans during this stage but talked little about these efforts.

Stage Three is the stage at which individual faculty make the leap to actual retirement. What seemed to motivate faculty members in Harris and Prentice's study (2004) to make the leap was financial incentives and specific incidents such as a bad teaching experience. Once the decision was made, individual faculty members reported a sense of relief and began communicating with others again. Finally, in Stage Four, the employee creates an "ex" role. Harris and Prentice report that the majority of their participants engaged in other income-producing roles shortly after retiring while also pursuing hobbies. Many, however, missed the classroom. Most continued to stay in touch with their campuses. Interestingly, in retirement, faculty continued to identify themselves as community college faculty members. Obviously, that role had become a major career identity for them. Although these findings are based on one qualitative study, they have implications for what community colleges can do to support faculty members in the retirement process as opposed to just letting them leave. Given the wave of current and impending retirements, this topic needs greater study.

Conclusion

A number of conclusions about the community college faculty career and labor market emerge from this review. Becoming a community college faculty member may not be a person's initial career goal but may result instead from viewing the position as a positive choice after working in other settings, inside or outside academe. Those who intend to become community college faculty members find that no official preparation is required other than receipt of the appropriate academic credential required for entry, which, depending on one's broad teaching area, may be a master's degree with eighteen hours in the teaching field or a baccalaureate degree or less in career and technical education fields. Typically, teaching experience or potential and fit with the community college mission is also preferred. Some indication has surfaced in recent years that community colleges prefer faculty candidates with doctoral degrees even though the narrow focus of a Ph.D. is seen as antithetical to the community college mission. Despite availability of Ph.D. candidates, the master's degree has had considerable sticking power as the primary required qualification for a community college teaching position. We do not see any change in the requirement of some related work experience for those teaching occupational-technical courses. Some teaching experience is preferred and is often a prerequisite for all candidates.

Relatively little is known about the labor market for community college faculty members and the search process by which they are selected. Existing research on the labor market suggests that community colleges hire their full-time faculty from a wide variety of sources appropriate for the various programs offered. Unlike research universities that rely on hiring newly minted Ph.D.s, community colleges draw their faculty from other community colleges, from secondary schools, from business and industry, and from four-year colleges and universities. In general, the little research on the topic suggests that colleges may advertise their faculty positions nationally but typically hire regionally if not locally. This approach has important implications for faculty recruitment.

The search process consists of recruitment, selection of candidates to be interviewed, the actual interview, and the selection of the preferred candidate.

Existing scholarship includes a concern for more active recruitment of faculty, efforts to standardize the process, and concerns about the lack of attention paid to the teaching ability of entering candidates. Once hired, faculty members face determination of their initial entering academic rank and salary, a probationary period, and retention through tenure or long-term contracts. Again, compared with our knowledge of faculty careers in research universities, we know little about important aspects of faculty careers in community colleges. In an effort to ensure that community colleges have adequate pools of highly qualified faculties, much more needs to be learned about the labor market and the search process that links potential candidates with community college faculty positions.

Institutional Factors Affecting Community College Faculty Work Life

MANY FACTORS INFLUENCE THE WORK OF faculty members in community colleges. Chief among them are institutional mission and students served. Although the community college's broad curricular mission to provide occupational, general education, and transfer courses affects the programs offered, it is its societal mission of open access and the curricular limitation of course offerings to the first two years of postsecondary education that most affects faculty work. Open access results in an enormous range of students in every respect: age, ability, race or ethnicity, and motivation in attending. Some students choose the community college as a place to take just enough occupationally focused courses to get a job. Those who intend to earn a baccalaureate choose to take their general education courses for a low rate of tuition at a nearby community college. Still others use the community college as a place to learn English as a second language or earn a GED. Many students take courses to make up for academic deficiencies. Others merely want to engage in lifelong learning.

Unlike most of their colleagues in four-year colleges and universities, community college instructors have little say over who comes to study in their college or who shows up in the classroom. Clark (1987) views this lack of authority over who enters the classroom as one of the great challenges of teaching in a community college, one of the factors that work against professionalization of the community college professoriate.

Another important factor is that community college faculty members are restricted to teaching first- and second-year or lower-level courses because of the institution's focus on the first two years of college. Faculty members teach the courses over and over again and, unlike their counterparts in four-year colleges and universities, have little choice over the courses they teach. Clark (1987) and others have argued that being restricted to lower-division courses in their area of specialty is a reason the master's degree is preferred as the entry credential for community college faculty members. A high degree of disciplinary specialization is not necessary. In addition, the institutional focus on teaching leads to high teaching loads, typically five courses per semester. Research is neither expected nor rewarded.

In their recent book, Levin, Kater, and Wagoner (2006) suggest another force is affecting community college faculty members. They argue that the institutional context for community college faculty work is shaped less and less by the mission to serve students and increasingly by a need to serve both the local and global economies. In their view, community colleges are increasingly instruments of business and industry through provision of short-term training programs that generate revenue and through adoption of efficiency and accountability measures characteristic of business. Further, they argue that these trends are affecting the work of traditional full-time arts and sciences or transfer faculty as well as occupational faculty members. Although it is not our purpose in this monograph to discuss in detail the missions (or the changing missions) of the community college, no doubt exists that the overall or dominant mission—and the role of faculty in carrying out that mission— also affects the conditions and nature of faculty work. This chapter examines several specific institutional factors that affect faculty members in community colleges. In particular, we examine faculty participation in institutional decision making through collective bargaining and shared governance, and departmental organization.

Background

Two-year colleges have historically been considered to be much more bureaucratic than four-year colleges and universities. This perspective partly reflects the development in the 1950s and 1960s of "a pyramid structure for governance ... in which power flowed from the president at the top of the organization through layers of staff—vice presidents, deans, directors, department heads, and faculty" (Alfred, 1994, p. 247). In this organizational structure, "faculty maintained primary responsibility for decisions on courses, curricula, and matters that affected teaching and learning, whereas administrators maintained responsibility for decisions related to planning, coordination, and allocation of resources" (p. 247).

As the community college grew and became more established, conflicting interests on the part of faculty, administrators, and students resulted in unionization on the one hand and the growth of shared governance through faculty senates on the other (Alfred, 1994). Often the distinction between the two forms of governance is not clear in the literature. It is not always clear whether authors are talking about unions, senates, or both. Some authors undoubtedly use the terms interchangeably. Faculty members typically engage in shared governance through senates. Whereas faculty associations in the form of unions set up a potential adversarial relationship between management and employees, shared governance operates from the perspective that the college "belongs" to its constituents, all of whom should be involved in decision making.

Increasingly, either in the shared governance framework or external to it, the last decades of the twentieth century witnessed yet another form of participation in organizational decision making: the rise of management techniques premised on the notion of greater participation in decision making. One widely used technique in community colleges is Total Quality Management (TQM), or its more recent designation, Continuous Quality Improvement (CQI). These techniques provide nonadversarial ways to become involved in governance (Alfred, 1994). The ideal scenario, according to Alfred, is one involving faculty and staff in institutional decisions broadly, including planning and budget as well as curriculum. Unfortunately, the literature suggests that Alfred's ideal is far from realized.

Surprisingly, we found little research on the involvement of faculty in CQI. What little literature is available on the topic is from the early to mid-1990s. It may be that these processes, as they rely heavily on committees and teams, are considered to be the same as the normal shared governance processes.

We argue that emerging forms of faculty governance (over and beyond bargaining units) are one indication of increasing professionalization of community college faculty, although we will review some counterarguments later. For the purpose of this chapter, we define governance as "the process for locating authority, power, and influence for academic decision among internal and external constituencies" (Alfred, 1985). Given this broad definition, community college faculty members participate in institutional governance in a number of ways. They do so as members of a department or division, through institutional task forces and committees, through collegewide governance structures such as senates, and through collective bargaining (Case, 1985). We focus on collective bargaining and on faculty senates, as the most has been written about these two forms of participation.

Collective Bargaining

Collective bargaining emerged in community colleges in the 1960s with the unionization of Henry Ford Community College in Michigan (Cunningham, 1983–84). The earliest work stoppage by community college faculty took place at that institution in 1966. Between 1966 and 1983, fifty-one work stoppages occurred lasting an average of twenty days (Cunningham, 1983–84).

The pace of unionization greatly increased in the 1970s and 1980s as individual states passed legislation to allow public employees to unionize (Cohen and Brawer, 2003; Deegan, Tillery, and Associates, 1985). No history is available of how and why community colleges, as they were founded and developed, tended to form collective bargaining units (unionization and community college growth roughly coincide temporally). Deegan, Tillery, and Associates (1985) suggest that "over time, the [union] contract became an acceptable way of responding to faculty interests in the welfare of their institutions and participation in their governance" (p. 17). To the extent community and junior colleges were linked to local public school districts, unionization may have been an extension of unionization of public school teachers.

Cohen and Brawer (2003) report that in 1998, approximately 60 percent of community colleges were unionized. Estimates of the number and percentage of faculty covered by bargaining agreements are conflicting. According to Cohen and Brawer (2003), the contracts covered 110,000 faculty members. Rhoades (1998) reports that 94 percent of public sector community college faculty members are represented by bargaining units (p. 12). An analysis of faculty in the NSOPF:04 data suggests that Rhoades's estimate is too high. Over half (58.4 percent) of the faculty responding to NSOPF:04 were members of unions, while 30 percent reported that unions were not available on their campuses (Kent Phillippe, AACC, personal communication, July 20, 2006). Based on these conflicting data, all we can assume is that between 60 percent and 90 percent of community college faculty members work in a unionized setting.

Holding 54 percent of the 344 contracts in 1998, the National Education Association (NEA) is the dominant bargaining agent for community colleges (Cohen and Brawer, 2003; Rhoades, 1998). Note that one contract may cover an entire state community college system. NEA is followed by the American Federation of Teachers, with 32 percent or 110 contracts, and the AAUP trails, with only nine contracts (Cohen and Brawer, 2003). Despite initial fears that the collective bargaining unit would supplant faculty senates (see Rubiales, 1998), it apparently has not happened.

As might be expected, a flurry of writing appeared on unionization and its effects in the 1970s. Since then, the issue of collective bargaining and its effects on faculty have been nearly absent in the literature. This absence suggests to us that community college trustees and administrators have come to terms with unions and have learned how to deal with them. Where unions exist, they have become part of the normal working of institutions. As Cohen and Brawer (2003) suggest, once faculties vote to unionize, they rarely vote to reverse their decision.

What precisely do unions do and what influence do they exercise? As Rhoades (1998) notes, unionization is about more than improving wages. It is also a strategy to restrict managerial control over work conditions or conversely to gain a larger faculty voice in control over the conditions of their work. According to Ernst, as quoted in Cohen and Brawer (2003), union contracts "include contract management procedures; rights of bargaining agents (as well as defining who is in and out of the bargaining unit); governance items such as personnel policies and grievance procedures; academic items such as class size and textbook selection; economic benefits; and working conditions such as parking facilities and office space" (Cohen and Brawer, 2003, p. 134).

Rhoades in his 1998 book, *Managed Professionals,* provides the most recent in-depth look at union contracts and their effect on faculty work. Interested in faculty autonomy on the one hand and managerial direction on the other, Rhoades calls faculty "managed professionals" (p. 4) because of what he sees as increasing administrative efforts to control faculty. As he points out, the colleges and universities that are unionized are not the ones that are usually studied. He uses a national database of union contracts to study the degree to which unionized faculty have autonomy or not. Rhoades examines several important aspects of faculty life to determine the extent to which the faculty or administration has control over faculty work: rewards, retrenchment and reorganization, part-time faculty, technology and outside employment, intellectual property, and control over one's own time.

Rewards

Rhoades (1998) looked for evidence of three aspects of salary structures: merit, market, and equity. One of the main effects of union contracts is on salaries of community college faculty members. It comes as no surprise that two-thirds or 69 percent of the 137 two-year college contracts he looked at use a salary schedule. Rules or criteria for placement on the schedule include education, experience, degrees, graduate courses, to a lesser extent participation in faculty development, and seniority (p. 42). Of contracts at two-year schools, 69 percent based placement or adjustment on degrees, 64 percent on credits earned, and 29 percent on publications. Only twelve contracts used performance as a criterion for placement on the salary schedule. Moreover, the set salary schedules of two-year colleges were not likely to include rank. Rhoades calls these factors certification-based proxies for merit as opposed to a merit-pay model. Although the merit pay model is often presumed to be a marker of greater professionalization, he points out that merit pay models actually give greater control to managers to the extent merit is determined by administrators such as department chairs.

In the contracts Rhoades (1998) reviewed, community colleges were less likely than four-year institutions to include market as a basis of salary adjustment. That is, community college contracts are less likely to respond to the supply and demand for faculty members in their offering salaries. The way in which community colleges do respond to market is by adjusting placement on the salary schedule, which is controlled by salary schedule rules. Although this situation may be changing in response to the need for faculty in high-tech fields, no documentation exists of it in the published literature.

Very few two-year college contracts address racial or gender equity in hiring. When they do include equity provisions, the purpose is to assure greater equity among salaries rather than the difference implied by merit systems. Rhoades (1998) concludes, "Indeed, equity provisions may be less commonly found in the contracts of two-year institutions because they are less necessary given the existence of standard salary indexes" (p. 71).

Retrenchment and Reorganization

A majority of the two-year and technical college contracts Rhoades (1998) examined provide rationales for retrenchment of faculty. Financial exigency was a stated rationale for only 9 percent of contracts, whereas other economic reasons, academic reasons, and student demand were cause for layoffs in 60 percent or more of the contracts with rationales for retrenchment. Other economic reasons do not typically rely on dire financial crisis to justify layoffs. Rather, the contracts used language such as financial "reasons" and "considerations" (p. 99). Academic reasons included program elimination and discontinuation. Student demand-based rationales are more common in two-year colleges than in four-year college contracts and include vague language such as "changing," "declining," or the slightly more specific "major decline" (p. 101). Rhoades points out that in some two-year college contracts, the wording is designed to allow layoffs for either a general decline or decline in a specific program. He did find a few community college contracts that use more specific language to define temporally the period under which the decline would be determined (p. 102).

Examining the extent to which faculty members are involved in retrenchment decisions, Rhoades (1998) found that less that one-third of two-year college and technical college contracts had provisions for faculty involvement in decisions to lay off faculty. Potential forms of involvement included consultation, meetings and discussion, and committee involvement. Of the community colleges that did have provisions for faculty involvement, consultation was the most frequent (nineteen of forty-seven contracts).

Under union contracts, managers are also subject to various constraints on firing or laying off two-year college faculty members. They include rules of order establishing priority for categories of faculty (whether part time or full time) and specifying whether notice must be given and if so how much. Almost all contracts with rules of order use seniority in category and layoff unit to determine layoffs. Other provisions specify reassignment or retraining and provisions for reemployment. Overall, Rhoades found that two-year college contracts were less likely than four-year college contracts to have provisions for rules of order, notice, reassignment, and recall. It would appear that constraints on managerial discretion in laying off faculty members are less prevalent in two-year institutions, thus giving managers more power.

Given the prevalence of part-time faculty at two-year colleges, it is useful to examine to what extent they are included in contract provisions. What Rhoades (1998) found is not encouraging for part-time faculty members. Only 20 percent of contracts in both two-year and four-year colleges had any provisions for the appointment or release of part-time faculty. Managers had a great deal of discretion to hire and fire part-time faculty members, and faculty members have little involvement or say in the matter. When the contracts did mention layoffs, the provision typically specified that part-time faculty would be laid off before full-time faculty members. Very few contracts had collective workforce provisions that limit the number or proportion of part-time instructors. Only a few years later, Levin, Kater, and Wagoner (2006) found that almost half of collective bargaining agreements did include part-time faculty members. The authors did not specify what aspects of part-time faculty life are covered by these contracts, however.

Two-year college contracts are more likely than those of unionized four-year colleges and universities to provide rights and benefits such as insurance and leaves to part-time faculty (Rhoades, 1998). Their duties are relatively undefined in either sector, with the exception of evaluation and office hours. Rhoades argues that the rights afforded part-time faculty members run counter to the stereotype about working conditions in academe (that working in a four-year college is better than in a two-year college). Faculty claims on property and autonomy are greater in two-year contracts. He also found that in the area of ownership of intellectual work, four-year and two-year institutions are equally likely to have provisions. In other words, when there is a relationship between institutional type and contract provisions protecting faculty (ownership, autonomy, profits), it is in the expected direction of favoring the two-year college faculty members (Rhoades, 1998).

What Rhoades (1998) does not examine is the extent to which contract provisions affect life on campus. Are unionized faculty members more satisfied and more productive? Are their salaries higher than those in nonunionized campuses? Cohen and Brawer (2003) argue that unions raise salaries initially but that their influence tends to level off, resulting in no or limited salary differences between unionized and nonunionized faculty salaries. Given the local nature of the community college faculty labor market, a number of factors influence faculty salaries, with perhaps the most important being the wealth of a community college district in states with local funding. Two-year colleges are less influenced by a national market—the need to keep up with the Joneses—than other types of colleges and universities. On the other hand, a finding of no difference between unionized and nonunionized salaries suggests that institutions do mimic each other to some extent. According to Cohen and Brawer (2003), a few studies (which they do not cite) have suggested that faculty members are more satisfied on nonunionized campuses with respect to involvement in governance, workload, and recognition, but few such studies exist.

Finley (1991) conducted one such study, examining selected public two-year colleges in the North Central Association of Colleges and Schools. He found that the only dimension on which unionized faculty were more satisfied than nonunionized faculty was on remuneration, and even there the difference was not significant. As a consequence, Finley questioned why unionized two-year colleges continued to maintain unionization, as it did not seem to make unionized faculty members more satisfied in their job than those in nonunionized settings. Moreover, there seems to be little evidence that the salaries of unionized faculty members are higher than those of nonunionized ones.

Overall, we can conclude that unions are quite prevalent in community colleges, affecting upward of 60 percent of full-time faculty in this sector. Some changes have occurred over time in bargaining matters, from issues of salary to personnel matters (Levin, Kater, and Wagoner, 2006). Although providing some protections for faculty autonomy and control, the provisions of these contracts give administrators considerable control over faculty life.

Faculty Involvement in Shared Governance

If there is little current attention to unions and their effects on faculty, there is even less discussion of faculty involvement in shared governance. In addition to bargaining associations, there are two aspects of faculty involvement in decision making in community colleges. The traditional way for faculty members to be involved is through some form of senate or shared governance process. Levin, Kater, and Wagoner (2006) define shared governance as "the mechanism through which higher education's major stakeholders actively participate in the decisions that affect their lives within the campus community" (p. 47). Moreover, shared governance is "the organizational work in public community colleges [that] is shared between faculty and administration" (p. 50). The second way for faculty members to be involved in decision making is through processes that may or may not be part of shared governance such as involvement in management teams.

Collins (2002), Lucey (2002), and Miller (2003) argue that a fit exists between the democratic rhetoric underlying the community college mission and the concept of shared governance. Miller (2003), summarizing previous research on the topic of senates at community colleges (much of it his own), concludes that senates do indeed exist at a majority of community colleges. From his own survey of sixty-six community colleges, he concluded that 72 percent had a faculty governance body. The vast majority of the respondents to Miller's survey were led by an elected leadership team; however, five reported administrative oversight. Although some faculty governance bodies included administrators, faculty, and staff, the vast majority represented faculty only. The governance bodies in his study dealt with a variety of issues, most of which were related to various aspects of faculty life (policies, workload, evaluation, contracts, and office hours, for example). They appeared to be less involved in planning and budget issues.

Although faculty senates existed in two-year colleges long before 1989, the shared governance model promoted by California Assembly Bill 1725, passed in 1989, is credited with being an excellent example of a new wave of faculty participation in shared governance. Collins (2002) notes that the bill "moved the colleges away from their K–12 roots, raised minimum qualifications for faculty, extended probation for new faculty members from two to four years, strengthened faculty evaluation through mandated peer review, and established expectations and funding streams for faculty professional development and curricular innovation" (p. 2). In addition, the legislation recognized local academic senates "as the bodies through which faculty would participate in governance, and it mandated that local boards of trustees consult collegially with these local senates" (p. 2). The bill is credited with encouraging many experiments and reforms, giving California community college faculty members responsibility for hiring, evaluating, and laying off faculty and for tenure review and professional development. Faculty members also have primary responsibility for academic policies, including degree requirements, grading policies, and curriculum (p. 2).

Collins (2002) notes, with some regret, that the California ideal has not been realized in full. Although some colleges have made the transition to effective shared governance, others have not. Obstacles include colleges that are hesitant to organize, lack of funding, and lack of appropriate preparation on the part of faculty members and administrators to participate in shared governance.

Although the statewide Academic Senate for California Community Colleges entered into a formal agreement with the AAUP to protect academic freedom and governance rights, business influences have increasingly come into conflict with faculty participation in governance. For example, some view corporate management fads such as CQI as attempts to dismantle faculty governance. On the other hand, management strategies such as TQM can be seen as an effort to get away from the top-down management characteristic of community colleges. These management techniques have been widely hailed as more democratic and involving, thus leading to more effective decisions and organizations with a greater sense of ownership for and commitment to decisions.

To some authors efforts to achieve accountability and efficiency also threaten faculty governance. For example, the emphasis on producing student learning seeks to remove faculty evaluation from the purview of faculty and place it in the hands of some "objective" measures of production. Management reorganization also favors full-time "managers" as opposed to faculty-appointed chairs (Levin, Kater, and Wagoner, 2006; Rhoades, 1998).

Little research has been conducted about perceptions of community college faculty members regarding faculty involvement in shared governance or decision making at their institution. One such study was conducted by Thaxter and Graham (1999), who sought to determine the extent to which faculty members in Midwestern community colleges were involved in decision making. Based on survey results, they found that the only real area of involvement faculty reported was related to course content and curriculum. That is, faculty members were substantially involved in student outcomes assessment and developing the curriculum for academic programs. Of some concern is the finding that faculty members have "little sense of involvement in the institution outside of the classroom, such as institutional goal-setting, recruiting or evaluating personnel, or contributing to the budgeting process" (pp. 668–669).

Thaxter and Graham (1999) indicated that the majority of faculty members rated their administration as a 4.4 on a scale of 1 (autocratic) to 10 (team oriented). This rating suggests that most of the faculty in their study saw their administrators as being more autocratic than not. Many respondents amplified their numerical ratings with comments. The largest group of comments (twenty-two out of fifty-six) considered their administrators "outright dictatorial" (p. 666) individuals who intentionally excluded faculty members from decision making. Smaller numbers of comments described administrators who were genuinely team oriented (16 percent of the fifty-six comments), administrators who sought input but did not give authority (7 or 12 percent of comments), administrators who gave the appearance of wanting faculty involvement but acted differently (5 or 9 percent of fifty-six comments), and administrators about whom faculty had a wait-and-see attitude (5 or 9 percent) (p. 667).

Not surprisingly, we get a slightly different take on shared governance from presidents. In a national study of community college presidents and faculty senate leaders, Pope and Miller (2000) found that presidents tended to agree that bureaucratic and democratic structures can coexist and that hearing from many voices strengthens participatory decision making. The presidents also tended to believe in shared decision making and in faculty as their equals. Interestingly, presidents tended to feel less strongly that these attitudes were learned through participation in faculty governance. In contrast, faculty senate leaders reported stronger beliefs in shared governance and thought that the faculty senate provided a good learning experience for faculty.

The scholarship about institutional governance indicates little to no discussion of the relationship between bargaining units and the faculty senate. Levin, Kater, and Wagoner (2006) believe that centralization of decision making in community colleges through collective bargaining has expanded rather than limited faculty participation in governance. They found that more than half of community college collective bargaining agreements "outlined a process for faculty participation in traditional areas of shared governance such as curriculum and faculty evaluation, areas of primary faculty responsibility as suggested by the AAUP/ACE/AGB" (p. 54). The primary areas of shared governance included in agreements were curricula, evaluation, grievances, sabbatical leaves, and retrenchment decisions. Only one-fourth to one-half of the contracts they examined included specific language for faculty involvement in "hiring, disciplinary hearings, calendar, tenure, professional development, and budget decisions" (p. 55). Contracts were silent on who is involved in issues such as the developing and securing of new faculty positions, program changes, management hiring, budget, professional development, tenure, faculty hiring, discipline, calendar, and curriculum.

Most writers about shared governance in community colleges view faculty participation in shared governance as a good thing. Participation is believed to contribute to ownership and commitment. Proponents of shared governance think that it should be spread and strengthened in community colleges (e.g., Collins, 2002; Pope and Miller, 2000). One question is whether, given the opportunity, community college faculty would seize a more active role in community college management and governance. The California experience (Collins, 2002) suggests that it may not be the case.

In contrast, Levin, Kater, and Wagoner (2006) suggest that faculty participation in governance furthers management, not faculty, interests in increasing productivity, accountability, and efficiency. From this view, managers want to increase faculty participation so that faculty members share the workload, thus increasing productivity. They note that almost half the colleges with bargaining units provided for involvement in areas that the authors consider outside the traditional responsibility of community college faculty members: calendar, grievances, and discipline—evidence of new managerial trends and the concomitant decline in meaningful faculty involvement. All of it is exacerbated by legislative calls for accountability and use of performance funding. The market economy and resulting competition for resources behind this emphasis on productivity and efficiency have resulted in increased cooperation between faculty (labor) and administration (management), albeit in Levin, Kater, and Wagoner's view (2006), for less-than-ideal motivation. In lieu of increased monetary rewards, management (administration) offers the promise (or requirement) of participation in shared governance. They call it the "commodification of cooperation" (p. 49). In this scenario, "the activity of faculty participation masks the substantive nature of this participation: relegated to areas that do not and cannot affect the significant institutional outcomes of who is served and the substance of education and training, faculty are de-professionalized, cogs in the corporate educational wheel or gear" (p. 137). Moreover, faculty members have a "diminishing influence on matters that count: their expertise and professional judgment are discounted" (p. 138). This insight led the authors to conclude, "We now question whether shared governance in the community college is an academic ideal [that] upholds the professionalization of the workforce or a neo-liberal activity imposed by management to foster efficiency and effectiveness by engaging faculty in management work" (p. 61).

Although Levin, Kater, and Wagoner (2006) make a compelling case that faculty are not involved in a meaningful way in decision making, we question whether this phenomenon is new. Scholars have long seen community colleges as top-down organizations in which administrations play a dominant role. What is different about Levin, Kater, and Wagoner's argument is that what other scholars see as a good thing (increasing involvement in shared governance), they see as a plot to further disenfranchise faculty by coopting them to do management's dirty work. Their perspective that shared governance as manifested in the union contracts they studied may serve to deprofessionalize community college faculty members is further examined in the next chapter. We also note that a considerable body of literature is critical of shared governance in four-year colleges and universities as well (see, for example, Tierney, 2004).

Other Institutional Factors

Other factors also affect faculty work in community colleges. In addition to administrative prerogatives in community colleges and how faculty participation in institutional decisions is circumscribed as a result, another factor of some import is the academic department or division.

Academic Departments or Divisions

Departments tend to be defined by academic discipline or area. As knowledge has grown and become more specialized, the number of departments has grown. In four-year colleges and universities, the department is the basic organizational structure, the place where academic work is organized and packaged and where faculty are nurtured and evaluated. According to Cohen and Brawer (2003), the department or division is also the academic building block of community colleges. In community colleges, the department or division is "organized around a cluster of academic disciplines or related teaching fields" (p. 129), and they see departments in community colleges as a means of creating manageable divisions of work more than as intellectual homes for faculty. They suggest that smaller institutions are more likely to have larger (and fewer) units or divisions encompassing multiple disciplines, whereas larger colleges may have a larger number of departments built around one discipline or teaching area. Collective bargaining may have influenced the move from departments to divisions to reduce the number of department chairs classified as administrators under the bargaining scheme (Cohen and Brawer, 2003).

Although Cohen and Brawer (2003) suggest that the influence of departments is quite substantial, little has been written about departments in community colleges and what they do. The only book-length study is the work of Seagren and others (1994), who conducted a national study of community college department chairs and their departments. The authors found the following characteristics of academic departments (or instructional units, as Seagren and others call them):

1. The average department or instructional unit had eleven to twenty faculty members.
2. Over half were departments while 36 percent were divisions.
3. Nearly half (49.9 percent) had ten or fewer part-time faculty, 20 percent had eleven to twenty part-time faculty, and 10 percent had twenty-one to thirty part-time faculty.
4. Campuses had, on average, eleven to twenty department chairs.

Seagren and others (1994) found that an overwhelming majority of department or divisional chairs thought that the following roles were important: planner, information disseminator, motivator, facilitator, visionary, advocate, delegator, conflict resolver, resource allocator, mentor, evaluator, and negotiator. The researchers placed these roles into three clusters: interpersonal role, administrator role, and leader role.

In another study of department chairs, Hammons (1984) classified the duties or roles of chairs (and thus functions of departments) as administration, relations with students, resource acquisition and allocation, management of faculty, and curricular and instructional tasks. Judging from these roles, the department is a place where faculty work is facilitated, faculty members are mentored, and faculty needs advocated for. It is also a place where faculty are evaluated and given the resources to support their work. Departments, through the chair, motivate faculty and help faculty to plan for the future. More specifically, departments are the focal point of developing programs, scheduling classes, and securing part-time faculty. New full-time faculty members are typically selected by committees of departmental or divisional faculty, limiting the role of administrators in the hiring process.

Unfortunately, departments may not be as successful at nurturing faculty members and promoting the college's mission as desired. Grubb and Associates in their 1999 study of community college faculty found that community college faculty members are quite isolated and have few opportunities to come together to talk about teaching in any meaningful way. Although the researchers do not discuss the role of departments specifically, it may be that faculty members' isolation and lack of teaching culture is the result of the relatively weak role of departments in community colleges.

Connections with Occupational Field

Grubb and Associates (1999) suggest that various occupational fields may influence the work of faculty teaching in related programs. Little has been written about this topic, but occupational programs often have advisory groups from the field to help them maintain personal contact with the field of practice and to receive advice on academic programs. The influence rarely extends beyond that of programmatic advice, but the mere fact that academic programs in occupational and vocational fields are influenced by demands of the occupation serves to influence faculty work.

Extrainstitutional Factors Affecting Work Life: Legislative Actions

Honored but Invisible (Grubb and Associates, 1999) discusses how legislative mandates and policies from funding—or lack of it—to unfunded mandates such as accountability affect faculty work. Our purpose here is not to repeat these authors' excellent analysis of how external factors such as funding affect teaching but to say that funding affects everything from institutional mission to class size to support for teaching to employment of faculty. Many of these points have been touched on elsewhere in this monograph. For example, Levin, Kater, and Wagoner (2006) see the norms of the global economy pressing community colleges to be lean and mean, catering to business and industry, and preferring employees or forcing faculty to do administrative work. From our review, we conclude that the influence of state and federal policies on community college faculty work deserves much greater research attention than received to date. In viewing the community college as a local or regional institution, we may overlook the system forces affecting it.

Pressures for accountability also affect faculty members at all levels of the higher education system. Accrediting bodies have, for a number of years, insisted that colleges at all levels engage in outcomes assessment to determine what students actually learn. The press to actually yield results will only be greater with the recent publication of the Spellings Commission report (U.S. Department of Education, 2006), *A Test of Leadership: Charting the Future of U.S. Higher Education.* Spellings urges greater transparency for higher education's accomplishments and accountability for student learning. How do these external mandates affect faculty work? We really know little about this subject. We make a rather false assumption that community colleges may "do assessment better" than four-year colleges and universities because they are teaching colleges in which administrators have more authority over faculty work than do their counterparts in four-year colleges and universities. But we really do not know. Although we are skeptical of national assessment mandates emanating from the federal government, we do agree that assessment is here to stay and that we need to know more about how it affects faculty work.

Conclusion

This chapter has examined several of the main institutional or organizational features of community colleges and their effect on faculty work. In general, it appears that administrators still retain considerable control over faculty work in community colleges. In fact, some signs point to an increase in managerial roles. Collective bargaining and participation in faculty governance are the two most common ways for faculty to circumscribe administrative authority. But even these two institutional features have their limitations. Collective bargaining cuts both ways. Although it circumscribes administrative prerogative on the one hand, it accords administrators considerable power on the other. Likewise, although faculty participation in shared governance is more prevalent now than in the past, there is some indication that this role has come at a price—the price of collaborating with administrators. We are not totally prepared to accept Levin, Kater, and Wagoner's vision (2006) of community college faculty members as willing participants in the institution's transformation from a college devoted to student access and success into an instrument of economic development. We suggest that these goals are not mutually exclusive—and never have been. That is, rarely, if ever, has higher education in the United States been devoted to learning for its own sake; it has always been tied to economic development objectives for individuals and for the country. Although it is true that faculty activities are increasingly circumscribed by managerial concerns about efficiency and accountability, it is a concern affecting all of higher education and not just community colleges. With the exception of the influence of resources, notably absent from our discussion is literature on the effects of institutional policies on the part-time faculty.

Looking to the Future: The Status of Community College Teaching as a Profession

SCHOLARS WRITING ABOUT THE COMMUNITY COLLEGE have long been concerned about the professionalization of community college faculty members. Two questions seem to dominate: Is community college teaching a profession? If it is, is it a unique profession? This chapter discusses the concepts of professions and professionalization, reviews the perspectives on whether community college teaching is a profession, and speculates about the effects on a professionalized faculty of selected emerging issues facing community colleges.

Characteristics of a Profession and Professionalization

To examine this issue, it is helpful to review the characteristics of a profession. Sociologists who write about professions and the process of professionalization admit that the use of the word is varied and often confused (Abbott, 1988; Freidson, 1973, 2001). Although these scholars may not agree on the meaning and process of professionalization, most scholars agree that a profession has several key characteristics. For example, Larson (1977, p. x) argues that professions have a cognitive, a normative, and an evaluative dimension:

> *The list of specific attributes [that] compose the ideal-type of profession may vary, but there is substantial agreement about its general dimensions. The cognitive dimension is centered on the body of knowledge and techniques [that] professionals apply in their*

work, and on the training necessary to master such knowledge and skills; the normative dimension covers the service orientation of professionals, and their distinctive ethics, which justify the privilege of self-regulation granted them by society; the evaluative dimension implicitly compares professions to other occupations, underscoring the professions' singular characteristics of autonomy and prestige. The distinctiveness of the professionals appears to be founded on the combination of these general dimensions. These uncommon occupations tend to become "real" communities, whose members share a relatively permanent affiliation, an identity, personal commitment, specific interests, and general loyalties.

The cognitive, normative, and evaluative dimensions consist of such generally accepted characteristics as control over specialized knowledge and skill (Freidson, 1973), human problems as the object of professional work (Abbott, 1988), entrance gained only after a prolonged period of study and controlled by the profession itself, self-control exercised over work and evaluation of that work (Freidson, 1973), ethical codes of conduct to guide behavior, and self-regulation of the profession by other members of the same profession. Typically, members of professions are dedicated to doing good for their own satisfaction and for the benefit of others (Freidson, 1973). For Larson, professions are a political expression, compensating for subordination, individual powerlessness, and sometimes low pay. Professions (especially professions such as law and medicine) gain power from competence in abstract or esoteric bodies of knowledge and skills needed by society. Further, professions are identified by typical organizations and institutional patterns: professional associations, professional schools, and self-administered codes of ethics (Larson, 1977, p. x). According to Freidson (1973), gaining the right to control work is what really distinguishes professions from occupations. This power is contingent, however. Professions are subject to the power of state and other powerful benefactors. Nevertheless, the elite that sponsor the profession help to guarantee political and economic influence (Freidson, 1973, p. xii).

Although this list comprises commonly recognized characteristics of professions, in the real world professions seldom adhere to the professional ideal in its totality (Freidson, 2001; Larson, 1977). For example, Freidson suggests that the amount, length, theoretical level, and extent of specialization of training in the profession are rarely specified. The concept of "profession" is a social construct whose meaning is fluid and changes with the time and context.

Professionalization is the process by which members of the profession gain exclusive right to establish the aforementioned characteristics. Professionalization has also been described "as the process by which producers of special services sought to constitute *and control* a market for their expertise. Because marketable expertise is a crucial element in the structure of modern inequality, professionalization appears *also* as a collective assertion of special social status and as a collective process of upward social mobility" (Larson, 1977, p. xvi). Professionalization, then, is the process of translating one set of scare resources—knowledge and skill—into social and economic rewards (p. xvii).

Is Community College Teaching a Profession?

As stated earlier, the issue of faculty professionalization has been a relatively important topic for scholars writing about community colleges. The scholars who have tackled the subject have used different definitions of profession and professionalization. Garrison (1967), one of the first to discuss this topic in detail, employed the criteria of control over the characteristics and number of students, time available to do the job well, access to professional development, and connection or lack thereof with other faculty to assess professional status. Using these fairly traditional characteristics of professional work, Garrison concluded that community college teaching was not a unique profession.

Cohen and Brawer (1972, 1977, 1987) have been equally concerned about whether community college teaching is a unique profession, but they look at somewhat different indicators, ones built around instruction. Based on a number of faculty studies conducted between 1971 and 1984, Cohen and Brawer (1987) found limited progress in the professionalization of community college faculty. Some key indicators of professionalization they used in their various studies were self-management, independence, self-evaluation, and provision of distinct services to a unique clientele. In the 1970s Cohen and Brawer (1977) claimed, "The faculty feel powerless to change the conditions of their work" (p. 71). In their 1987 study of liberal arts faculty at community colleges, they found some characteristics of a profession: an increasing period of preparation for the position (a master's degree rather than a bachelor's degree), moderate control over entry into the profession, and some self-policing. They also noted, however, that faculty feel a great deal of professional loneliness (1987), a problem also indicated by Grubb and Associates (1999) in their study of faculty in thirty-two community colleges.

In their 2003 book, Cohen and Brawer indicated some positive trends, namely that the community college has become a well known and visible work site. Furthermore, "as a group, faculty members no longer look to universities for their ideas on curriculum and instruction, nor do they see the community colleges only as stations on their way to university careers" (p. 100). When they looked for institutional manifestations of professions such as unique two-year college faculty professional associations, journals, and grants for curriculum development work, however, they found few. The authors concluded, "Although instructors at two-year colleges may be moving toward the development of a profession, its lines are as yet indistinct" (p. 99).

Palmer (1992) argued that a new look was necessary in the late 1980s and early 1990s as community colleges sought to replace large numbers of retiring faculty members. In considering whether community college teaching is a profession and whether its practitioners are professionals, Palmer uses four frames of reference. The first frame, the institutional, speaks to the extent to which faculty members embrace the comprehensive curricular mission of the community college and the nature of its students. Palmer sees limited fulfillment of this perspective and argues that the advocates of this perspective "never structured it on a fully developed rationale that would link the perceived uniqueness of the community college to the practice of teaching" (p. 31). The legacy of the institutional perspective remains as one component of Clark's framework (1987).

The second or scholastic frame sees a broad definition of scholarship (including traditional research as well as the scholarship of teaching) as consistent with the mission and work of community college faculty. In fact, Palmer (1992) notes, "In embracing this broad definition, the scholastic frame of reference lays bare the false notion that research universities are the sole theater for scholarship in higher education" (p. 32). According to Palmer (1992), George Vaughn has argued for attention to scholarly activities, as he sees scholarship as related to effective teaching. Palmer's review of the research led him to conclude that most faculty do something defined as scholarship and think it helps with their teaching. They do not think scholarship should be required, however.

The third frame, the classroom research frame, suggests that the scholarship of teaching fits with the community college mission. Faculty professionalism could be anchored in classroom research anchored in action research. In other words, community college faculty members should be engaged in research on their teaching, which could become the hallmark of a unique community college teaching profession. Palmer's fourth and final frame (1992) is pedagogical. It is built around student outcomes and the ability of faculty members to effect change in students. Palmer concludes that saying teaching is the main focus says little about how community college faculty members define themselves as professionals.

What can be done to foster professional consciousness? For Palmer (1992), community college teaching has become a career, and now the challenge is for its practitioners to see themselves as professionals. Palmer concludes that preservice education and training have been of little use in fostering such a professional identity (although the national Preparing Future Faculty program offered at research universities now includes attention to faculty careers at a wider range of institutional options). The answer must come from within through an institutional culture that has high expectations of its faculty. Chief among these expectations is how the community college views its mission. Palmer (1992) argues that community colleges should focus not just on numbers of students served but also on ways in which clients are served or made better by experience. Moreover, all four frames of reference are essential to recognizing a professional identity among faculty.

Another effort to look at the professional status of community college faculty is Outcalt's work (2002b), in which he used the results of a national study of two-year college faculty members to test the definitions of community college faculty profession found in Garrison (1967) and Cohen and Brawer (2003). In the survey, faculty self-reported on a number of items directly or indirectly related to aspects of professionalism. Using Garrison's criteria, Outcalt concluded that community college faculty members still have not achieved control over who their students are or how many they teach. In addition, they lack sufficient time to do their jobs well. Although they do have access to professional development, it is often inadequate. Finally, community college faculty members often work in isolation and have little interaction with colleagues.

Community college faculty members fare no better when Outcalt's survey results (2002b) are juxtaposed against the Cohen and Brawer's criteria (2003). Rather than gaining ability to manage themselves, faculty had diminished capacity for self-management, according to Outcalt. This finding is supported by Levin, Kater, and Wagoner (2006) in their study of community college faculty. These authors perceived that faculty still have control over their instruction, defined broadly, but little control over other matters. Other studies of faculty participation in shared governance confirm this finding (Miller, 2003; Thaxter and Graham, 1999). Faculty members are committed to effective instructional practice, but Outcalt found little evidence of discrete services to distinct clientele. Outcalt concludes that divisions in the community college professoriate (liberal arts versus occupational faculty, part-time faculty versus full-time faculty) "have prevented it from achieving status as a separate professional group" (2002b, p. 158). He identifies several factors impeding professional identity: increasing prevalence of part-time faculty, increasing importance of the doctorate, and the expanding mission of the community college with the concomitant pressure on its faculty to be all things to all people.

Bayer and Braxton (1998) take a very different approach to the question of the professional status of community college faculty members. Noting that the existence of a code of ethics is one marker of a profession, they explore the extent to which community college faculty members have internalized norms about teaching. Bayer and Braxton argue that we must focus on norms because the profession of college teaching typically has no formal codified set of ethics. In this case, internalized norms function in the same way as a mechanism of social control. This study represents a significant shift in focus from the approach of Cohen and Brawer (2003), Palmer (1992), and others who have focused on disciplinary journals, associations, and other markers of commitment built around instruction.

Based on their national study, Bayer and Braxton (1998) conclude that a normative structure exists that is recognized among community college faculty members across disciplines. Specifically, they note several identifiable negative dimensions (unacceptable behaviors) to these norms: interpersonal disregard or disregard for opinions of students and colleagues, restrictive accessibility or refusal to participate in activities such as curricular planning, failure to meet classes on time or keep appointments, inadequate planning surrounding actual delivery of class, including not providing a syllabus on time and failure to order textbooks, practices perceived to result in unfair grading, and moral turpitude involving behaviors such as having sexual relations with a student or coming to class under the influence of alcohol (pp. 194–197). Women and those with doctorates tended to take a somewhat tougher line on violations of norms than faculty in the hard sciences.

As a result of their findings, Bayer and Braxton (1998) concluded that normative structures exist in community college teaching and that community college faculty members are more professionalized than previous research has shown. "Community college faculty members hold particularly high standards regarding teaching performance and related behavior" (p. 201). What the researchers also acknowledge is that we have no evidence of the extent to which faculty actually adhere to or violate the norms identified. We only know from this study what they believe to be the norms and standards for proper behavior.

From this research, we can conclude that at least one aspect of professionalism does exist, but as Bayer and Braxton (1998) note, more work needs to be done on whether and to what extent other dimensions of professionalism are present such as the mastery of an abstract body of knowledge and what that relevant abstract body of literature is.

A number of community college scholars whose work is reviewed in this monograph (for example, Cohen and Brawer, Palmer) have argued that instruction is the content around which the community college profession should develop to make it unique. In contrast, McGrath and Spear (1991) and Spear, Seymour, and McGrath (1992) strongly object to the notion of instruction's becoming the focus around which the profession of teaching is developed. They argue that effective instruction cannot be divorced from disciplinary knowledge and pedagogy and that the community college needs a surrogate for the university's strong disciplinary culture to ensure professional growth after graduate school. In their view, for this growth to flourish the intellectual and cultural environment in which community college faculty practice must be supportive. It seems unlikely to us that mastery of instruction as a body of knowledge is sufficient in and of itself to constitute a profession that would distinguish community college teaching from high school teaching.

Burton Clark, in his seminal work, *The Academic Life: Small Worlds, Different Worlds* (1987), identifies characteristics along which the academic profession can be differentiated, depending on institutional type. Clark's approach is distinct in that he compares faculty members at various types of colleges and universities. As summarized in Twombly (2005), Clark identifies the characteristics of the academic profession as follows:

Research is the defining characteristic because it gives professors the ability to define parameters of their own work such as what they teach, whom they teach, and what they investigate. Administrative control is the alternative.

One's disciplinary base provides the core for faculty identity and exerts a strong influence on faculty work.

Difference and hierarchy are determinants of degree of professionalization. Such factors as commonality work against professionalization.

Institutional and disciplinary characteristics exert a strong influence on the nature of professionalization because some institutions emphasize teaching and others emphasize research.

Belief and commitment are important characteristics of academic professionals. The extent to which faculty identify with their institutions or with their disciplines is important for Clark, who is also interested in specific ideologies such as the unfettered search for truth or belief in students' success.

There is a high degree of authority to control work.

There is a promise of a career.

Disciplinary associations play an important role.

Clark's ideal professional (1987) is unabashedly based on the standard of the research university. Not surprisingly, community college faculty members do not fare very well when compared with this ideal. According to Clark, community college faculty members are "positioned at the extreme" (p. 203) and are closer to high school teachers than university professors in terms of professional characteristics. More surprising is that his conclusions are not that far from those of Cohen and Brawer (2003) and Outcalt (2002b). Clark (1987) says, "Astute observers have argued cogently that community college faculty are not in a position to follow the cosmopolitan road to professionalism so heavily traveled by university professors: 'The community college faculty disciplinary affiliation is weak, the institutions' demands for scholarship are practically nonexistent, and the teaching loads are too heavy for that form of professionalism to occur'" (p. 243). In addition, he finds that community college faculty members have little control over their work or their students. He does, however, find stronger commitment to what he calls an "anchoring ideology" (belief in open access and success for all students) than he finds among faculty at some other kinds of colleges and universities.

With Clark's criteria (1987) of the academic profession as a framework, Twombly (2005) used her study of searches to examine the extent to which community college teaching is a profession. She argues that faculty hiring offers a window into key aspects of faculty professionalism. As other studies have shown and we have discussed in this monograph, the period of preparation for entering the profession has increased from the days in which the bachelor's degree was sufficient. The period of preparation is shorter than necessary for other professions and for the same profession in other types of colleges and universities that require faculty to have doctorates, however.

Community colleges, almost by definition, do poorly on Clark's hierarchy and difference criterion (1987). Twombly (2005) found that the colleges have a formulaic hiring process, starting salaries are typically set by a negotiated salary schedule, and there is little educational and experiential difference among candidates. Searches typically identified many candidates who meet the minimum criteria. Teaching promise becomes the main criterion, and it is hard to differentiate. A typical assessment of teaching is based on previous teaching experience or a short (fifteen- to twenty-minute) demonstration to the hiring committee. Moreover, the community colleges in her study did not appear to be competing with other colleges for the same candidates.

Academic work for community college faculty is clearly teaching. One dean in Twombly's study (2005) described community college work as "real teaching," as opposed to some other kind of teaching attributed to universities. One cannot conclude, however, that advanced preparation in pedagogy (or "instruction" as Cohen and Brawer [2003] might call it) has become the norm. Research, defined as the discovery of new knowledge, is not disparaged; it simply is not promoted. In fact, a lengthy publication list might make search committees skeptical. Discipline did play an organizing role in searches in that search committees typically comprised faculty who teach in the area. Successful candidates were expected to have at least eighteen graduate hours or a master's in the teaching discipline. Twombly argues that community colleges take a "soft" disciplinary approach to hiring instructors, particularly in small, rural colleges where faculty have to teach subjects related to their field.

Although not all who write about and work in community colleges would agree (see McGrath and Spear, 1991; Spear, Seymour, and McGrath, 1992), the anchoring ideology of the profession appears to be commitment to learning and success of all students. This ideology is espoused by new faculty as well as hiring committees.

With respect to authority to hire their own colleagues, Twombly (2005) found that community college faculty members have more than high school teachers but less than university professors in almost all respects of their job. Clearly faculty have a greater role in job searches than do high school teachers but may not be as concerned about participating in searches as are research university faculty. The role of faculty in the final selection decision also varies, depending on the particular community college, whereas in research universities faculty members almost always have more authority than administrators. In unionized institutions, faculty members have some authority in setting the salary schedule through their role in the bargaining units. Although Clark (1987) sees unions as working against professionalism, faculty associations do give some leverage as discussed in greater depth in the previous chapter (see also Levin, Kater, and Wagoner, 2006; Rhoades, 1998).

As for the promise of an academic career, the evidence is mixed. Although the new faculty members interviewed for Twombly's study (2005) considered the community college a legitimate work site that they intentionally sought, they had not foreseen community college teaching as a career goal when they began graduate school. This finding is confirmed by Fugate and Amey (2000) in their study of faculty career stages and by Wolf-Wendel, Ward, and Twombly (2007) in their study of community college faculty mothers with young children. These women, some with Ph.D.s, indicated they intentionally chose to teach in a community college because they thought it would be easier to balance family and work there than in a four-year college or university. Another measure of "promise of career" is the extent to which faculty members who enter can get tenure, move up in the rank system, and either stay at one college or move to another. As indicated in the earlier discussion of community college faculty careers, a large percentage of full-time community college faculty members seem to easily get permanent appointment status, whether that is called tenure or not.

Twombly (2005) concludes that the career of a community college faculty member unfolds differently from the career of a research university professor but maybe not so differently from a faculty member at other types of colleges and universities. Although community college teaching falls down on some of Clark's characteristics (1987), it does exhibit some characteristics of a profession: that of college teaching practiced in a specific site. Twombly concludes that the question is not whether they are professionals but how they are professionals and how the institution socializes them to be the kind of professional community colleges need.

In contrast, Levin, Kater, and Wagoner (2006) paint a grim picture of an increasingly managed faculty subject to an institution that is placing entrepreneurial market activities over and above the traditional mission of the community college. In this scenario, faculty members in all academic sectors are losing control over their work, but community college faculty members may be more adversely affected than others because they begin from a point of less autonomy. Faculty members have become workers in a corporate culture. Although they participate in decision making, Levin, Kater, and Wagoner (2006) argue that the participation masks the nature of the decision making. Their research suggests that faculty participation is "relegated to areas that do not and cannot affect the significant institutional outcomes of who is served and the substance of education and training. Faculty members are de-professionalized cogs in the corporate educational wheel or gear" (p. 137). In this sense community college faculty members are experiencing what all other academics are. Faculty have an opportunity in a *nouveau college* to "chart incremental change in redefining their role and status as professionals" (Levin, Kater, and Wagoner, 2006, p. 134).

The authors portray community college faculty members as having some professional agency with respect to defining their futures. Indications of this trend are increasing preference for the Ph.D. in some institutions, equity for the part-time labor force, the opportunity for faculty members to be more knowledgeable and assertive in negotiating working conditions to assure alignment with professional roles, and the assumption of more control over the use of technology. The authors believe that faculty members need to be more aggressive in positioning themselves—in other words they need to be more assertive in governance and about more issues than salaries. Part of professionalization for the community college professoriate also involves determining its role in economic development. They suggest that in redefining the role of the community college faculty as professionals, teaching and learning should remain the mainstay or core function and as such "mediate student learning" (Levin, Kater, and Wagoner, 2006, p. 141).

In sum, the evidence about the extent to which community college teaching is a profession is mixed, depending on which characteristics are used to define a profession. Although some authors focus primarily on professionalism with some comparative in mind, the comparison group is often not made explicit. What some authors have argued more recently is that professions conform to the characteristics of the ideal profession to a greater or lesser extent.

Following this line of argument, the question is not so much whether community college teaching is a profession but *how* it is a profession, that is, what does it mean to be a community college instructor? And how are new members, most of whom did not set out to become a community college faculty member, socialized to the values and commitments of the profession?

Here we come back to Larson's definition (1977) of a profession cited at the beginning of this chapter. She argues that occupations become professions when they become communities whose members share values, an identity, interests, affiliations, and loyalties. This definition suggests that we might look at some different markers of professions in the community college professoriate. Specifically, how do people become members of the community? And how is a sense of identity and commitments and loyalties fostered?

Our review leads us to conclude that there is little evidence that community college teaching is a unique profession. Palmer (1992) and Vaughan (1986, 1988) provide models of what such a unique professional identity based on the scholarship of teaching might look like. Unfortunately, Grubb and Associates (1999) show that a professional identity built around teaching did not exist in community colleges in the late twentieth century.

Nevertheless, evidence suggests that community college teaching exhibits some characteristics of a profession. In fact, Clark (1987) found that community college faculty members were more committed to an anchoring ideology than faculty members in some other types of colleges and universities. As Larson (1977) and Freidson (1973) suggest, professions vary in the extent to which they match the ideal characteristics of a profession. Educators are the same: they vary in the extent to which they meet the ideal characteristics of a profession by the type of institution where they teach. Community college teaching clearly lies somewhere on a continuum between public school teaching and research university professing. The professional characteristics of community college teaching (for example, entrance requirements) and their place on the professional continuum are determined by the unique mission and other circumstances that shape faculty life, not because community colleges are failed research universities.

We argue that scholars and community college administrators should focus attention on sharpening the role of community college faculty members around which their professional identity is built and then on how new faculty members are socialized to this professional identity. Clearly progress along these lines has been made since the emergence of the community college as an appendage of the high school. As Grubb and Associates (1999) show, however, there is much room for further development.

Possible Future Influences on Faculty Professionalization

We begin our discussion of the future of the community college professoriate with the assumption that community college teaching is a profession in the sense that teaching is a profession and we accept that community college teaching exhibits more characteristics of a profession than does high school teaching and less than university teaching. Certain interesting institutional developments are occurring, however, that may influence the future of community college teaching as a profession and the professional status of those who dedicate their careers to this work. Two of the most significant are the emergence of the community college baccalaureate (Floyd, Skolnik, and Walker, 2005) and the potential emergence of what Levin, Kater, and Wagoner (2006) call the *nouveau college*. The first may exert an influence on the qualifications and preparation necessary to become a full-time faculty member. The second has the potential to have conflicting impact on the professional status of community college teaching.

The Community College Baccalaureate

Community colleges in at least twelve states as of the writing of this monograph have been authorized to award the baccalaureate degree. Although this phenomenon has escalated in the last decade, it is not new to the public two-year college. Farnsworth (2006) details how what used to be called Joplin Junior College in Missouri developed a baccalaureate program in the 1960s and by 1965 was granted baccalaureate status by the legislature. Almost four decades later it received university status as Missouri Southern State University. Nevertheless, it continues to offer some career education associate degree programs. So also does Missouri Western State University, which began as St. Joseph Junior College in 1915, became a four-year institution in 1969, and then became a university in 1977 (Farnsworth, 2006). Certainly a number of private junior colleges in the first half of the twentieth century developed four-year degree programs while offering two-year programs and eventually became four-year schools. What is different about the current spurt of two-year colleges receiving authorization to award the baccalaureate is that there is an orchestrated effort to promote what is called "the community college baccalaureate," typically thought of as a baccalaureate degree awarded by the community college. Indeed, an organization, the Community College Baccalaureate Association, was established in 1999 to promote and support the community college baccalaureate and more recently "access to the baccalaureate degree on community college campuses" (Community College Baccalaureate Association, 2004) through such means as 2 + 2 baccalaureate degree programs at community college campuses (Townsend, 2006).

The rationale for developing baccalaureate programs in community colleges is twofold: the institution's doing so is an extension of efforts to provide access to higher education, including the baccalaureate. The community college baccalaureate is also framed as an effort to meet the workforce development needs of local communities in areas such as nursing or teacher preparation in which there is a shortage. Its proponents contend that many community college students would like to earn a baccalaureate degree but are unable to transfer to a four-year institution to do so. They may be hindered in transferring because the four-year school will not accept many of their credits, because the four-year school's costs are too expensive for them, and because the four-year college is too far away geographically for them to commute regularly and still hold a job and take care of their families (Burke and Garmon, 1995). Besides wanting to help these students more easily obtain a bachelor's degree, the community college is more willing than most four-year colleges to develop a baccalaureate in applied areas such as manufacturing technology. A state's local and state businesses leaders would like to employ individuals with baccalaureate degrees in these areas, so the community college is serving area workforce development by offering the degrees (Walker, 2001; Wallace, 1999). A recent added rationale is Walker's argument (2006) that offering the baccalaureate is "a means of serving the requirements of the twenty-first-century knowledge-based world of globalization" (p. 14).

In the late 1980s and early 1990s, promotional efforts for what has been called the "community college baccalaureate" (Floyd, Skolnik, and Walker, 2005) stressed that only applied baccalaureate degrees would be developed (Burke and Garmon, 1995). More recently, community colleges have sought to offer baccalaureates in programs typically offered by four-year schools, programs such as nursing and education. The rationale here is that four-year schools have insufficient capacity to educate all the students who seek these degrees and are unwilling to increase their capacity, so community colleges will meet local workforce needs by offering the programs.

The community college baccalaureate is not without controversy. Some regard it as an inferior degree that may hurt its recipients in the job market and in efforts to enter graduate programs (Eaton, 2005; Wattenbarger, 2000). Others contend it is a form of mission creep and a major step in community colleges' turning into four-year colleges. Indeed, almost all community colleges authorized to award this degree have become four-year colleges. For example, Westark Community College was authorized in 1979 as the only public two-year college in Arkansas to develop a baccalaureate program. By 2002 it had become the University of Arkansas–Fort Smith (Farnsworth, 2006). The regional accrediting body for educational institutions in the southeastern United States, the Southern Association of Colleges and Schools, initially required that all schools awarding a bachelor's degree must become a four-year college with a name change reflecting their new status. In other words, they could no longer be called "community colleges," but "by early 2006, SACS ... had softened its position" and granted two Florida community colleges "the right to keep 'community' in their respective college names" (Floyd, 2006, p. 62), although they are four-year schools.

Two-year colleges that have recently become four-year schools after they were authorized to award bachelor's degrees acknowledge they are four-year schools but some maintain they are still committed to their two-year programs. Thus St. Petersburg College, the first community college in Florida to receive legislative authorization to award a baccalaureate degree, states on its Web site that it is a four-year institution but that "the college's commitment to its two-year curriculum, which has earned it wide recognition and annually wins it high national ranking, remains as strong as ever" (St. Petersburg College, 2006). In so doing, institutions may be trying to counter critics' contention that baccalaureate programs will lead to a decreased focus on the student for whom the community college is the only resort academically and financially. Neglecting its open access mission and the consequent developmental education curricular mission could result from diversion of institutional resources and energy to baccalaureate programs and the possibility of rising costs to students to cover these new programs.

From the faculty's perspective, community college baccalaureates mean that more faculty members with doctorates will need to be hired to staff these programs. How will this step affect community college faculty members? Will the community college develop a two-tiered faculty, with the top tier consisting of doctorate-holding faculty who teach upper-division courses in the baccalaureate programs and the lower tier of master's-level faculty who teach lower-division courses only? Will there be a difference in salary scales for these two tiers? Will there be an increased push for all community college faculty members, not just those teaching in the baccalaureate programs, to conduct some form of scholarship? Indeed, will scholarship be required and rewarded?

Should the answers to the above questions be "yes," it would appear that community college faculty as a whole would be seen as more professionalized because more possess the doctorate. Faculty groups, however, such as career faculty members teaching in areas poorly rewarded in the labor market (such as child care) might be judged in the institution as less professional than other faculty. Although some elements of this attitude already exist as evidenced by tensions between transfer and career education faculty members, this attitude may increase, prompted by the institution's new focus on baccalaureate programs.

In a related vein, career education faculty members face the requirement of increasing entry credentials because of rising interest in the transfer of students in career education programs, especially the A.A.S. degree. Once labeled as "terminal education" (Townsend, 2001), the A.A.S. degree now serves as the pathway to the baccalaureate for a number of students, especially in programs whose graduates are highly sought in the workforce (such as manufacturing technology). The limited research on these students shows that A.A.S. degree recipients in general do as well or better academically as students who transfer with the A.A. degree, although A.A.S. recipients do not receive the baccalaureate at quite the same rate. Their longer time to degree may stem from their being employed in the area of their associate degree at the same time they are working on the baccalaureate. It may also reflect that not all the A.A.S. courses transfer or transfer as readily as do courses in A.A. programs (Townsend, 2001).

Although four-year schools are increasingly willing to accept courses in the two-year college major as upper-level major courses (Townsend, 2004), the courses typically need to have been taught by a faculty member with a master's degree because of requirements of regional accrediting bodies. Thus career education faculty in at least some programs will need to obtain a master's degree so that they can teach courses that will be accepted by four-year schools.

In sum, the development of the community college baccalaureate and the push to count A.A.S. courses and degrees as transfer-level courses are events likely to raise the required entry credential for career education faculty members and to increase the number of community college faculty members with doctorates. Given that a prolonged preparation time is one hallmark of a profession, these developments will likely lead to perceptions of greater professionalization of community college faculty. Additionally, with more faculty members possessing doctorates, interest may be greater in community college faculty conducting scholarship defined as original research.

Nouveau College

The impact of developments associated with what Levin, Kater, and Wagoner (2006) call *nouveau college* is somewhat less clear. On the one hand, they describe community college faculty as "worker bees" (p. 138) or cogs in the neoliberal version of the community college, a version that they see increasingly losing its focus on access and student success to a more management-driven focus on efficiency and profitability. On the other, they see an evolving professional definition for community college faculty. They offer the important perspective that the very definition of professionals is a social construction that is continually evolving. Thus they point out that there is a "spectrum in the professional role of faculty [that] varies contextually by institution, geographical location and organizational structure" (p. 138). From this perspective they are quite positive about the professional status of community college faculty. In agreement with other authors cited earlier, they see the trend of some community colleges, especially those adding a bachelor's degree, to increasingly hire faculty members with doctorates as one indication of professionalism. They also see the trend of offering benefits and improved working conditions to part-time faculty as a positive evolution in the professional role of community college faculty.

Equity for part-time faculty members is a controversial issue. One could argue that it works against the professional status of full-time community college faculty members. As we have seen, part-time faculty tend to have lower educational qualifications, less training, primary commitment to another job, or teaching commitment to several colleges simultaneously. To recognize this group with benefits then would seem to work in the opposite direction in terms of professionalization. The other way to think about it is that part-time faculty members are here to stay as a group. Their use is likely to increase and it is in the best interest of the profession, the community college, and its students to do everything to bring part-time faculty into the professional fold.

Control over working conditions is one area where Levin, Kater, and Wagoner (2006) see community college faculty members losing ground in their nouveau college. To the extent that autonomy and control over working conditions are indicators of professionalism, community college faculty would seem to be in danger. Although the majority of community colleges have faculty senates or bargaining units, the evidence presented earlier in this monograph seems pretty clear that these groups have relatively little control over matters outside the curriculum and the actual process of teaching. Levin, Kater, and Wagoner (2006) argue, and we agree, that community college faculty as professionals can and should be more involved and demanding when negotiating working conditions.

Additional challenges to the professional status of community college faculty members are the increasing uses of information technology and pressures to participate in economic development activities. We argue that such issues face faculty in all types of colleges and universities, not just community colleges. Nevertheless, the effects of technology on the nature and independence of faculty work are only beginning to be recognized and need to be monitored closely. Given their mission, community college faculty members may be particularly vulnerable to the negative influences of technology on professional autonomy, although as Rhoades (1998) notes, community colleges tend to be more progressive in terms of ownership of intellectual property than are four-year unionized faculties.

The press for faculty members to participate in economic development activities, whether directly related to offering courses for business and industry or merely engaging in entrepreneurial activities to raise discretionary dollars to replace disappearing public funds or support "extras," affects faculty in all colleges and universities. Again the mission and strong management orientation of community colleges may result in this trend's having a potentially bigger effect on community college faculty members.

Conclusion

Whether or not community college teaching is a profession is a question that has driven much of the early discourse about those who teach in two-year colleges. We argue that "What are the characteristics of community college teaching as a profession?" is a more appropriate question than "Is community college teaching a profession?" A review of characteristics of a profession and the concept of professionalization indicate that community college teaching evidences typical characteristics of a profession to a greater or lesser extent. We do not view community college teaching as a unique profession but as one that finds itself in a middle position on the continuum of teaching as a profession between high school and university teaching. It occupies this middle position not because of weaknesses of the community college or the individuals occupying faculty positions but because of the mission of community colleges and the nature of their students. Attention needs to be paid to how community college faculty members perceive their identity as members of the teaching profession and how these faculty are socialized to a professional identity.

Several current and future factors influence the professional identity of the community college professoriate. A major one is the development of what has been termed "the community college baccalaureate," a bachelor's degree awarded by the community college. As more community colleges are authorized to award this degree, required entry credentials for community college faculty members as well as expectations of them to be scholars (defined as those who contribute to the knowledge base of their teaching area) may change. Entry credentials for career and technical education faculty may also be raised as more students with the A.A.S. degree, traditionally a nontransfer degree, seek transfer to four-year schools.

The conception of the community college as nouveau college, an institution less focused on student access and success and more focused on its place in the market, may also influence the professional role of community college faculty. On the one hand, they may function as dronelike workers in an institution devoted to efficiency and cost savings. On the other hand, they have the potential to become more professional as they assume a greater role in their institution's governance.

A major challenge to the professional status of the community college professoriate is the high percentage of part-time faculty members. Although the reasons for their extensive presence are varied, the major one is cost savings, as the low cost of a community college education compared with other educational institutions is one of the major reasons for high enrollments in community colleges. It is therefore unlikely that the percentage of part-time faculty will decline much in the coming decades. Perhaps what needs to be addressed is ways to increase the professionalism of part-time faculty without detracting from that of full-time faculty members. It is this group of faculty who need to take a greater role in governance to ensure they have sufficient control over conditions affecting their work roles, including the use of technology in teaching and pressures to participate in economic development activities.

A Fresh Look at Community College Faculty

THIS MONOGRAPH HAS REVIEWED THE LITERATURE on community college faculty to construct a comprehensive picture of who they are, what they do, what the dimensions of their careers are, what the institutional factors affecting their identity and role are, and what the future of community college faculty as a profession may be. Our ultimate goal is to propose a fresh look at the community college professoriate.

For much of the late twentieth century, discourse about community colleges has posited them as an alternative institution, outside the mainstream of higher education institutions, in marked contrast to universities, and with a substantially lower status in the academic hierarchy. This view, which relegated junior and community colleges to the bush league or even academic Siberia (Caplow and McGee, 1958, p. 118), had led prominent scholars such as historian Frederick Rudolph (1977) to say about the community college: "In its rejection of national norms, cosmopolitan values, academic credentials, traditional standards, and professionalism, as well as in its embrace of the local, parochial, anti-intellectual, and familial, the community college ... may have placed itself beyond consideration, except in a limited sense, as a college" (p. 285). A far more recent example of this same kind of discourse is a statement by Pascarella and others (1998) about how community college administrators and student affairs professionals may have to "focus particular effort on eliminating the aura of second class status often attached to community colleges and their students in American society. ... This second-class or second-best mind-set may never be quite overcome, either by the students who enroll, or by the professional counseling staff who work at community colleges" (p. 191).

These views of the community college as an institutional type have permeated the research about those who teach in community colleges. Fiol-Matta (1996), herself a community college faculty member, acknowledges the low status of the community college but states that "this status has been conferred as much by misconception of the task of the community colleges as by the elitism of the higher education system" (p. 3). Because many people view the community college as concentrating on workforce development, its academic/transfer faculty members, "unlike their colleagues in the applied vocational fields, are often perceived as lesser scholars" (p. 3). Yet she sees changing perceptions of working in the community college as more of its faculty members possess doctorates.

Authors who write about community colleges attempt to legitimize the institution by trumpeting it as a teaching college with success for all students as its main mission and teaching as the main job of its faculty. The implication is that faculty members in community colleges are expert teachers, contrasted with faculty members at universities, who are presumed to be more concerned with research than teaching. Although not all agree that those who teach in community colleges are excellent instructors (see Grubb and Associates, 1999), in general they are portrayed as better teachers and more committed to teaching than are university professors.

One result of this discourse is the maintenance of the perspective that community college faculty members are lacking or inadequate in comparison with university faculty members. The teaching role is stressed for community college faculty and the research role for university faculty. Individuals who teach in community colleges are assumed to be experts in teaching, but it is a lower-status activity than research, the expertise of their university counterparts. Hagedorn (2004) suggests it is so because most authors on community colleges are university faculty members: "Because much of the literature regarding community colleges has been written from the perspective of elite universities, community colleges [and their faculty members] appear distorted and substandard" (p. 1).

It is not only university-focused researchers and sociologists who portray community college faculty members and community colleges in a negative light. One of the more surprising findings from our research for this monograph is that many scholars of the community college—even those who have made their careers and reputations as advocates (such as Arthur Cohen, Florence Brawer, Norton Grubb, and John Levin)—are quite critical of community college faculty members. Perhaps it is a natural phenomenon following on the almost missionary zeal with which community colleges have been portrayed positively and uncritically.

A number of recent developments, both internal and external to community colleges, call for reimagining the faculty role in community colleges. One development that argues for bringing the community college professoriate into sharper focus is the increased prominence or importance of the community college in preparing this nation's college-educated individuals. Over the last decades of the twentieth century and surely into the future, the community college has become the critical entry point to higher education for millions of students, particularly those from historically underrepresented groups. Given the critical role the twenty-first-century community college serves in providing college access to a widely diverse group of individuals and as it enters new educational territory through such offerings as baccalaureate degrees and alternative teacher certification for postbaccalaureate students, we must begin to understand community colleges and their faculty members on their own terms rather than as deficient universities and deficient faculty. The community college has finally arrived in the sense that it is widely acknowledged as an important component of the higher education system. It employs a considerable number of faculty members who must be better understood. At the same time it is time to reenvision the faculty as more than just failed four-year college and university faculty members.

Another development is the emergence of the community college baccalaureate. Clark's pronouncement (1987) about the community college— "No matter how much it may wish to be otherwise, the two-year college is junior, restricted, in the grade structure, to the work of the freshman and sophomore years and the awarding of a two-year degree" (pp. 58–59)—no longer holds true. Community colleges in several states are now authorized to offer the baccalaureate degree (Floyd, Skolnick, and Walker, 2005; Townsend, 2006). Indeed, some community college presidents even advertise their institutions as the new graduate schools, given the increase in postbaccalaureate students now attending community colleges (Townsend, 1999). In other words, the mission of the community college is changing so that some of these institutions now provide a level of education once restricted to four-year institutions.

As part of this development, community colleges authorized to award the baccalaureate will likely need to hire more faculty with the doctorate so that these faculty can teach the upper-division courses necessary for the baccalaureate. Typically the doctorate is seen as the credential certifying that an individual has the capability to conduct original research or Boyer's scholarship of discovery (1990). Faculty members with doctorates bring different training and perspectives to their work than do faculty members with a master's degree or less. To the extent that the community college baccalaureate further encourages the hiring of faculty members with Ph.D.s, the development of the community college baccalaureate may have an effect on faculty role.

Less positive are the trends brought on by increasing control of higher education, community colleges included, by internal administrators and external forces, be they the global economy or state and federal calls for accountability for student learning. The collective result is faculty members who are managed professionals constrained by administrative prerogatives and the demands of efficiency brought on by the global economy.

In light of these trends, what should the role of full-time community college faculty members be? We argue that the standard or stereotypical definition of a faculty member as someone who conducts research, teaches, and participates in disciplinary and institutional service is inadequate and inappropriate for the community college of the twenty-first century. Inevitably, application of this standard definition has led to the perception that anyone whose faculty position does not include all three roles is somehow a lesser or inferior faculty member. This standard definition of faculty roles is cumbersome and inappropriate when viewing the work of community college faculty members.

Because the traditional definition of faculty work as teaching, research, and service is so engrained in our conceptions of faculty work, it is difficult to imagine other possibilities. Our goal in attempting to reenvision the work life of community college faculty is not so much to get it right but rather to encourage others to continue the work.

Teaching is clearly the centerpiece of faculty work in community colleges and so it should remain. Although teaching is the agreed-upon emphasis of the community college, there is considerable evidence that teaching is not given the attention it deserves, given its primary place in the community college. The work of Grubb and Associates (1999) clearly points to the need for community colleges to pay more attention to teaching and to make a sincere commitment to doing it well. Part of taking teaching seriously, we believe, involves adopting Boyer's view (1990) of the scholarship of teaching. Boyer defines the scholarship of teaching as paying attention to teaching through thinking about what to teach and how to teach it and through maintaining currency in one's teaching field—whether it be auto mechanics, manufacturing technology, or American literature. We believe the scholarship of teaching undergirds all the work of faculty in the community college. To teach well, they must conduct the scholarship of teaching. Although most may not articulate participation in this kind of scholarship, it is what they intuitively do as they prepare for classes and seek to engage students in learning.

In taking this position, we agree with scholars such as Jim Palmer, George Vaughan, Arthur Cohen, and Florence Brawer, who argue that community college faculty should be experts in the scholarship of teaching. This is not to say that traditional research should be discouraged, only that the scholarship of teaching should be expected. This form of scholarship can result in several forms of products: papers for traditional journals, presentations at conferences, or assessment data for accountability purposes, courses, and program improvement. As the press increases on higher education to demonstrate what students are learning, all faculty members will be called on to engage in some form of the scholarship of teaching. Community college faculty members are well positioned to take the lead in developing good models of how to do this.

Service to their college and its local community will continue to be important for community college faculty members. In fact, we argue that they must become more involved in college governance and management. Although their doing so risks the charge that faculty are becoming administrative pawns and doing their dirty work, we argue that the alternative is worse. One characteristic of being a professional is having control over the conditions of one's work. No one will give this authority to faculty freely; faculty must want the responsibility, even demand it.

Our vision of community college faculty for the twenty-first century is not that dramatically different from what now exists. What is different is that we argue that community college proponents should not apologize for this conception of faculty work. Faculty members who do this work and do it well provide a service to hundreds or even thousands of students at their own institution. In the aggregate, the community college faculty provide a service to millions of students, many of whom are among the most vulnerable educationally. It is noble work and should be seen as such.

Challenges in Understanding Community College Faculty

In this volume we have tried to portray who community college faculty members are and what they do. In deriving this portrait, we have faced several challenges. One challenge is simply the high percentage of part time faculty members. Given that the majority of community college faculty are part time, a legitimate question arises: About whom are we speaking when we talk about "community college faculty"? Despite the numerical prominence of part-time teachers, the bulk of the research about two-year college faculty members is about those who are full time, particularly academic and transfer faculty. As a result, our view of the community college professoriate is somewhat distorted and incomplete. Although we described part-time faculty members as best we could and presented research findings about them, there was little research about them to present. Thus the portrait of the community college professoriate that can be most accurately drawn is that of its full-time faculty members, even though they represent only about 30 percent of all community college faculty members, albeit 30 percent who teach a majority of students.

Another challenge is the nature of the available research. The research on the community college professoriate is characterized by few book-length studies. With the exception of Grubb and Associates' *Honored but Invisible* (1999), Outcalt's *A Profile of the Community College Professorate, 1975-2000* (2002b), and Levin, Kater, and Wagoner's *Community College Faculty: At Work in the New Economy* (2006), the book-length studies are at least twenty years old. Journal-length articles are often based on local or small-scale studies. One of the things that surprised us is that those who do investigate and write about community college faculty tend to pursue the same topics repeatedly, creating a horizontal knowledge base—a lot of studies about a few topics—and studies that pursue the same questions in perhaps different settings without developing a deeper knowledge base that builds on itself. Finally, it comes as no surprise that scholars of community colleges contribute to the marginalization of the institutional type and its faculty members by publishing primarily in journals targeted to an almost exclusively community college audience. This strategy has the advantage of presumably reaching a practitioner audience in a position to apply findings from the research, but the result is that research-based knowledge of community colleges is rarely viewed by those working in four-year colleges and universities.

Specifically, we were struck by the lack of information about a number of topics critical to a complete understanding of the community college professoriate. As we reviewed the literature, we became aware of the many areas in which research about community college faculty members was lacking. In addition, our review of the available literature led us to other questions essential to developing and maintaining a high-quality community college faculty for the future. We offer a brief description of some of these areas with the hope that other researchers will work to close the gaps in the portrayal of community college faculty. The answers to these questions are important not only for providing a fuller picture of these faculty members but also for ensuring a faculty adequate to the existing and emerging missions of the community college.

Job Search and Labor Market
Like all educational institutions, community colleges are facing a wave of retirements and the need for new hires. To maximize their ability to find high-quality faculty members, we need to learn much more about the labor market for community college faculty. We know that it works significantly differently from that for research university faculty, but beyond a relatively few studies focused on specific aspects of the labor market and the job search

process, we know little about how job searches for these individuals occur, where faculty members come from, and how the labor market works. Related to a better understanding of the faculty labor market, we need to better understand how community colleges manage the ratio of full-time to part-time faculty members and how they decide when to fill a position with a full-time faculty member. Given the gap between the percentage of minority faculty members compared with the percentage of minority students enrolled at community colleges, it would also be helpful to understand the extent to which concerns for hiring faculty of color influence job searches and the efforts of community colleges to recruit these individuals.

Unlike the situation for prospective faculty in research universities, there is little guidance available for individuals interested in obtaining faculty positions in community colleges. Understanding the process from a candidate's perspective as well as from an institutional perspective would be useful. How might prospective faculty members better position themselves in a search? What characteristics would be attractive to a search committee, and what is the likelihood of obtaining a position if one is not from the state where the community college is located?

Additionally, the relationship of part-time positions to full-time ones is a potentially important question. Does holding a part-time position provide an advantage for an individual seeking a full-time faculty appointment? Additional research on the labor market for community college faculty members, the skills needed in being one, and the hiring process itself should help universities better prepare community college faculty members. In this way, the community college will be better able to attract individuals who not only want to work there but who are appropriately prepared to do so.

Tenure, Long-Term Contracts, and Promotion

Much has been written about the struggles of four-year college faculty in obtaining tenure and sometimes in being promoted to full professor, with particular emphasis on the problems of women and minority faculty (for example, Cooper, 2006; Garcia, 2000; Glazer-Raymo, 1999; Tierney and Bensimon, 1996). Yet almost nothing is known about the tenure and promotion process or the process of obtaining long-term contracts for community college faculty members. Perhaps little has been written because the process is not problematic. There are indications in the literature that obtaining tenure or long-term contracts is almost pro forma (Grubb and Associates, 1999). Yet is this portrayal fair and accurate? A recent study suggests that the tenure process may induce stress in at least some faculty members (Wolf-Wendel, Ward, and Twombly, 2007). This finding is somewhat surprising and merits additional research. If the process is pro forma and induces little stress, does the process need to be made more rigorous so as to increase the professionalization of community college faculty members?

Faculty Work Life for Particular Groups

Like faculty at any institutional type, the collective faculty can be disaggregated into particular subgroups by factors such as race and ethnicity, employment status (full time versus part time), unionization, and teaching area. We recommend that these subgroups or categories of faculty be researched in more detail. For example, some systematic studies of community college faculty of color might aid the institution in understanding how to better recruit these faculty members and what is satisfying and problematic about their work life. Some of these questions have been asked about women who teach in the community college (Townsend, 1995, 1998; Wolf-Wendel, Ward, and Twombly, 2007), and it is intriguing that they have not been raised, to our knowledge, about community college faculty of color. Overall, studies have shown that women in community college faculty positions are satisfied with their choice of workplace and with the work climate, partly because of the high percentage of women faculty members at the community college. Still we wonder whether the high percentage is a result of what we call "accidental equity"—equity in hiring achieved with no specific efforts or intention to do so (Townsend and Twombly, forthcoming). In using this term, we do not mean to imply that men or any other group has benefited from "intentional equity." We mean only that the high percentage of women faculty members has typically not resulted from particular institutional strategies to hire women. Certainly community colleges will have to work harder to attract faculty of color and to create satisfying work environments. To do so, we must understand better the current situation for faculty of color and what can be done to improve it.

Another group about which very little is known is vocational and occupational faculty members. Status differences between transfer and career education or vocational faculty and between developmental studies and "regular" faculty have been documented (see Grubb, 2005; Seidman, 1985) but not in any detail. Beyond these studies, we know almost nothing about this group of faculty, who serve a very important function in preparing a significant number of students for immediate employment. Yet because this group of faculty has heretofore not been seen as building a bridge for students to a four-year college or university, it has been ignored and devalued, perhaps even more than community college transfer faculty.

Yet another group that merits further research is part-time faculty. Qualitative studies of these faculty members could provide a richer picture of their life than is currently provided in national surveys. Disaggregating them by reasons for seeking employment in the two-year college and then ascertaining if differences exist in their perceptions of their role and their treatment in the institution could provide useful information for recruitment and professional development. And ascertaining what all types of part-time faculty members need for institutional support to be more effective faculty is a critical need, particularly given the extraordinarily high percentage of part-time faculty.

We also know virtually nothing about what community college faculty life is like for Ph.D.s fresh out of graduate school. Were they sufficiently prepared for the difference in institutional culture between community colleges and doctorate-granting institutions? Do they attempt to conduct research or was their decision to teach in the community college a deliberate decision to forgo research? What do they wish they had known about the community college before they decided to work there? Answers to these questions could lead to better efforts to prepare them for a position as a community college faculty member.

Related to these questions is a lack of knowledge about socialization of all community college faculty members to their jobs, regardless of whether they have a master's or Ph.D. or teach in transfer or vocational and occupational programs. The burden of this task seems to fall to faculty development programs. Our review of the existing research shows that faculty development programs are disappointing and that relatively little attention is given to developing a true teaching culture in community colleges. This situation seems inexcusable. Not only do colleges need to know what kinds of faculty development programs exist and who can participate, but they also need to know what works. Without such evidence, faculty development programs are at best a symbolic gesture to reinforce the community college's image as a teaching institution.

Faculty Governance

From an organizational perspective, it seems important to better understand faculty involvement in shared governance (for example, faculty interest and participation in institutional decision making). Levin, Kater, and Wagoner (2006) have provided us with a rather bleak perspective on faculty autonomy in the community college. Their work deserves further investigation, as forces they describe have the potential to affect everything the community college and its faculty do. Participation in faculty governance is an important indication of professionalization of the faculty as well as a potentially critical factor in the community college's future direction. These colleges have long been viewed as top-down, management-directed institutions in which faculty have little say. We argue that community college faculty members need to be actively involved in determining their future, whether through union or senate participation. Given the little research showing any benefit to unionization, we have to wonder whether faculty unions are the best means for faculty members to exert influence in community colleges.

In sum, a fresh look at the full-time faculty members who work in community colleges reveals them to be scholars who merit the respect of their colleagues in other institutional types and the esteem of the general public for their embracing the open door mission and their willingness to educate a highly diverse student body. Reasons they have not always received this respect include a lack of knowledge about them, a lack partly stemming from the high percentage of part-time faculty members who, as a group, have received almost no scholarly attention. The many part-time faculty who teach at community colleges also help maintain the institution's open door mission by educating its diverse students, keeping instructional costs low, and, in some instances, providing very current information about what is happening in rapidly changing fields of employment. We must acknowledge, however, that community colleges' escalating use of part-time faculty has possibly negative implications for the future of the community college professoriate as well as for the institution itself. The effects of such a high percentage of part-time faculty members clearly need to be researched.

Other needed research includes studies of the job search and labor market, the tenure and promotion process, faculty work for particular subgroups of faculty, and the faculty role in institutional governance. And we need more in-depth studies that are national in scope.

Conclusions

Although there is much we do not know about the community college professoriate, we have developed several conclusions about community college faculty members, whom we now deliberately contrast with four-year college and university faculty members to emphasize certain points.

What distinguishes two-year and four-year college faculty groups is not demographics but required educational credentials, which symbolize role expectations. Demographically these two groups of faculty are almost indistinguishable. Whether full time or part time, the typical faculty member in both the two-year and four-year sectors is white and middle-aged. The major difference is that two-year college faculty members are as apt to be female as male, unlike in the four-year sector, where male faculty members constitute the majority.

In terms of required educational preparation as indicated by entering educational credentials, the two groups differ greatly, and this difference is a manifestation of role expectations. The doctoral degree is required for most faculty positions at four-year institutions because its faculty are expected to be content experts or specialists at a minimum in their teaching and to possess the ability to conduct research, should it be required at their institution. In contrast, the master's degree is the highest degree required at the community college and is primarily required of academic and transfer faculty only. Some career education faculty possess only an associate's degree, although the majority possess at least a baccalaureate (Olson, Jensrud, and McCann, 2001). In fact, the diversity of required educational credentials among the community college professoriate is an unrecognized hallmark of this group.

As Clark (1987) has pointed out, the difference in required educational credentials for two-year and four-year faculty as groups is significant because not needing a doctorate marks community college faculty members as mere transmitters of knowledge, not as content specialists capable of conducting research in their discipline or field. Additionally, with the exception of the few institutions offering a baccalaureate degree, at most community colleges faculty members teach lower-division courses or courses offered in the first two years of a baccalaureate program. No more than a master's degree is thought necessary to have sufficient content knowledge to teach lower-division courses. By virtue of their teaching only lower-division courses, community college faculty members are seen as generalists rather than specialists in the content they teach. Additionally, receipt of the Ph.D. symbolizes fellowship in a national community of disciplinary experts. Without a doctoral degree, most community college faculty members would not be perceived as appropriate participants to provide service in national disciplinary organizations. Thus the potential to its faculty to have a national or cosmopolitan orientation versus a local orientation and reputation is limited by the community college's entry credential for faculty positions.

We question how relevant and realistic the issue of professionalization of community college faculty is. What is the benefit to the community college if its faculty members are currently seen as more professional than they were in previous years or if community college teaching is viewed as a profession?

As our review has illustrated, the question of whether community college teaching is a distinct profession has been discussed for several decades, with the discussion currently led by university professors. One issue in this discussion is the appropriate credential for community college faculty members. If we accept that raising the level of required entry credentials is not an economically feasible or necessarily appropriate way to claim that community college teaching is a profession (because of the limited labor pool of career and technical education as well as of part-time faculty), we could still claim community college teaching is a distinct profession if the required entry credentials included courses not required of four-year college faculty. Requiring its faculty to have courses in pedagogy would seem appropriate for an institution that claims to be a teaching college. The rub is that there is little evidence that college faculty with preparation in teacher training are any better (or worse) teachers than those without this training. Even if there were such proof, requiring pedagogical courses of all its faculty creates the same problem for the community college as would requiring a higher entry credential. The pool of candidates for both full-time and part-time positions would be considerably limited, thus hindering institutional capacity to serve students and probably raising instructional costs and thus tuition.

If the intent of the discussion about professionalization is not ultimately to alter status perceptions about the institution and its faculty but rather to improve the behavior of faculty members in their teaching-learning role, then their behavior needs to be examined in comparison with some nationally agreed-upon standards of professional behavior in college teaching. To our knowledge, no such standards exist. We do note that Bayer and Braxton (1998) found in their national study of community college faculty that they were more likely than four-year faculty to identify inappropriate teaching behaviors, suggesting a set of norms and standards for appropriate professional behavior.

Partly because of the issue of professionalization, we see the authority of some community colleges to award the baccalaureate degree as having the potential to create greater divisions among community college faculty members. Not only will it create a tier of faculty members who teach upper-division courses and a tier who do not, it also is possible that the divide between career education and academic/transfer faculty members will widen as academic/transfer faculty members potentially seek to align themselves with those teaching upper-division courses. The creation of the top-tier faculty will also exacerbate the difficulty of generalizing about the community college professoriate.

Unionization and the use of part-time faculty members are here to stay. The intersection of these two factors needs to be more closely studied. For example, to what extent does the increase in part-time positions fuel the development and maintenance of unions? Community colleges may be more affected by hiring part-time faculty members than are four-year colleges and universities, but the concomitant forces for change high-lighted by Levin, Kater, and Wagoner (2006) toward a managed profes-soriate affect all of higher education. Although community colleges may come out looking badly in their scenario, we note that it is all a matter of degree. No postsecondary sector is unaffected.

In sum, there is much that we do not know about the community college professoriate. This lack of knowledge may be one reason why its members have been and still are marginalized in discourse about the professoriate. We hope this monograph will serve as a stimulus for future research about this significant group of faculty.

Note

1. This question was apparently not asked in all the Murray studies, as it appears as an activity only in the national study (2001) and the Texas study (2000).

References

Abbott, A. (1988). *The system of the professions.* Chicago: The University of Chicago Press.

Adelman, C. (2005). *Moving into town—and moving on: The community college in the lives of traditional-age students.* Washington, DC: U.S. Department of Education.

Alfred, R. (1994). Research and practice on shared governance and participatory decision making. In G. A. Baker III, (Ed), *A handbook on the community college in America* (pp. 245–258). Westport, CT: Greenwood Press.

American Association of University Professors. (2006, March/April). *The devaluing of higher education: The annual report on the economic status of the profession, 2005–06.* Washington, DC: American Association of University Professors.

Antony, J. S., and Valadez, J. R. (2002). Exploring the satisfaction of part-time college faculty in the U.S. *Review of Higher Education, 26*(1), 41–56.

Avakian, A. N. (1995). Conflicting demands for part-time faculty. *Community College Journal, 65*(6), 34–36.

Bayer, A. E., and Braxton, J. M. (1998). The normative structure of community college teaching: A marker of professionalism. *Journal of Higher Education, 69*(2), 187–205.

Berger, A., Kirshstein, R., and Rowe, E. (2001, September). *Institutional policies and practices: Results from the 1999 National Study of Postsecondary Faculty, institution survey.* Washington, DC: Office of Educational Research and Improvement, U.S. Department of Education.

Blocker, C. E., and Wolfe, W. (1964–65). Academic rank in two-year colleges. *AACJC Journal, 35*(4), 21–25.

Boggs, G. (2004). Community colleges in a perfect storm. *Change, 36*(6), 6–11.

Bowen, H., and Schuster, J. (1986). *American professors: A natural resource imperiled.* New York: Oxford University Press.

Bower, B. L. (2002). Campus life for faculty of color: Still strangers after all these years? In C. L. Outcalt (Ed.), *Community college faculty: Characteristics, practices, and challenges* (pp. 79–88). New Directions for Community Colleges, no. 118. San Francisco: Jossey-Bass.

Boyer, E. (1990). *Scholarship reconsidered.* Princeton, NJ: Princeton University Press, Carnegie Foundation for the Advancement of Teaching.

Brewer, D. J. (1999). *How do community college faculty view institutional mission? An analysis of national survey data.* (ED 440 695)

Burgess, L. A., and Samuels, C. (1999). Impact of full-time versus part-time instructor status on college student retention and academic performance in sequential courses. *Community College Journal of Research and Practice, 23,* 487–498.

Burke, T. R., and Garmon, J. F. (1995). The community college baccalaureate. *Community College Journal, 65*(7), 35–38.

Burnstad, H. M. (1994). Management of human resources in the community college. In G. A. Baker III, (Ed.), *A handbook on the community college in America* (pp. 386–396). Westport, CT: Greenwood Press.

Campion, W. J., Mason, D. V., and Erdman, H. (2000). How faculty evaluations are used in Texas community colleges. *Community College Review of Research and Practice, 24,* 169–179.

Caplow, T., and McGee, R. J. (1958). *The academic marketplace.* New York: Basic Books.

Case, C. (1985). Supporting faculty leadership for change. In W. Deegan and D. Tillery (Eds.), *Renewing the American community college* (pp. 80–102). San Francisco: Jossey-Bass.

Cataldi, E., Fahimi, M., and Bradburn, E. M. (2005). *2004 National Study of Postsecondary Faculty (NSOPF:04) report on faculty and instructional staff in fall 2003.* NCES 2005–172. Washington, DC: Office of Educational Research and Improvement, U.S. Department of Education.

Chronicle of Higher Education Almanac. (2005, August 26). Vol. 52, No. 1.

Clark, B. (1987). *The academic life: Small worlds, different worlds.* Lawrenceville, NJ: Carnegie Foundation for the Advancement of Teaching.

Cohen, A., and Brawer, F. (1972). *Confronting identity: The community college instructor.* Englewood Cliffs, NJ: Prentice-Hall.

Cohen, A., and Brawer, F. (1977). *The two-year college instructor today.* New York: Praeger Special Studies.

Cohen, A., and Brawer, F. (1987). *The collegiate function of community colleges.* San Francisco: Jossey-Bass.

Cohen, A., and Brawer, F. (2003). *The American community college* (4th ed.). San Francisco: Jossey-Bass.

Collins, L. (2002). Shared governance in the California community colleges. *Academe, 88*(4), 36–40.

Colvert, C. C. (1952). The ideal junior college teacher. *Junior College Journal, 22*(9), 502–507.

Community College Baccalaureate Association. (2004). *It's about access.* Retrieved October 4, 2006, at http://www.accbd.org.

Cooper, T. L. (2006). *The sista' network: African American women faculty successfully negotiating the road to tenure.* Boulton, MA: Anker Publishing.

Cross, K. P., and Angelo, T. A. (1989). Faculty members as classroom researchers. *AACJC Journal, 59*(5), 23–25.

Cunningham, J. D. (1983–84). After a score of years, what's the faculty union score? *Community and Junior College Journal, 54*(4), 15–17.

Curtis, J. W. (2004). *Faculty salary and distribution fact sheet 2003–04.* Washington, DC: American Association of University Professors. Retrieved January 14, 2007, at http://www.aaup.org/AAUP/pubsres/research/2003-04factsheet.htm?PF=1.

Dee, J. R. (2004). Turnover intent in an urban community college: Strategies for faculty retention. *Community College Journal of Research and Practice, 28,* 593–607.

Deegan, W., Tillery, D., and Associates. (1985). *Renewing the American community college.* San Francisco: Jossey-Bass.

Diaz, V., and Cheslock, J. (2006). Faculty use of instructional technology and distributed learning. In J. Levin, S. Kater, and R. Wagoner, *Community college faculty at work in the new economy* (pp. 63–80). New York: Palgrave-Macmillan.

Dickinson, R. (1999). The changing role of community college faculty: Implications in the literature. *Community College Review, 26*(4), 23–37.

Dobrovolny, J. S. (1964–65). Preparation of junior college teachers of technical subjects. *Junior College Journal, 35,* 9–13.

Dolan, F. H. (1952). The preparation of junior college teachers. *Junior College Journal, 22*(1), 329–336.

Eaton, J. S. (2005). Why community colleges shouldn't offer baccalaureates. *Chronicle of Higher Education, 52*(1), B25.

Eckert, R. E. (1948). A new design for the training of college instructors. *Junior College Journal, 18,* 325–331.

Eells, W. C. (1936). Preparation of junior college instructors. *Junior College Journal, 7,* 55–56.

ERIC Clearinghouse for Community Colleges. (1994). *Community college faculty salaries.* EDINFO no. 4. Retrieved July 10, 2006, from http://www.gseis.ucla.edu/ccs/edinfos/edinfo4.html.

Farnsworth, K. (2006, June/July). Sliding up the slippery slope: The community college baccalaureate. *Community College Journal,* 8–11.

Finkelstein, M., Seal, R., and Schuster, J. (1998). *The new academic generation: A profession in transformation.* Baltimore: Johns Hopkins University Press.

Finley, C. E. (1991). The relationship between unionization and job satisfaction among two-year college faculty. *Community College Review, 19*(2), 53–60.

Fiol-Matta. (1996). Editorial: The community college in the United States: A profile of innovation and change. *Women's Studies Quarterly, 3* & *4,* 3–15.

Flannigan, S., Jones, B., and Moore, W. (2004). An exploration of faculty hiring practices in community colleges. *Community College Journal of Research and Practice, 28,* 823–836.

Flowers, L. (2005). Job satisfaction differentials among African American faculty at 2-year and 4-year institutions. *Community College Journal of Research and Practice, 29*(4), 317–328.

Floyd, D. (2006). Achieving the baccalaureate through the community college. In D. D. Bragg and E. A. Barnett (Eds.), *Academic pathways to and from the community college* (pp. 59–72). New Directions for Community Colleges, no. 135. San Francisco: Jossey-Bass.

Floyd, D., Skolnik, M., and Walker, K. (Eds.). (2005). *Community college baccalaureate: Emerging trends and policy issues.* Sterling, VA: Stylus Publishing.

Forbes, J. D. (1966–67). Research, teaching, and excellence. *AACJC Journal, 37*(4), 7–9.

Freidson, E. (1973). *The professions and their prospects.* Beverly Hills, CA: Sage.

Freidson, E. (2001). *Professionalism.* Chicago: University of Chicago Press.

Fugate, A., and Amey, M. (2000). Career stages of community college faculty: A qualitative analysis of their career paths, roles, and development. *Community College Review, 28*(1), 1–22.

Gahn, S., and Twombly, S. (2001). Dimensions of the community college faculty labor market. *Review of Higher Education, 24*(3), 259–282.

Gappa, J. M., and Leslie, D. W. (2002). Part-time faculty: Competent and committed. In C. L. Outcalt (Ed.), *Community college faculty: Characteristics, practices, and challenges* (pp. 59–68). New Directions for Community Colleges, no. 118. San Francisco: Jossey-Bass.

Garcia, M. (Ed.). (2000). *Succeeding in an academic career: A guide for faculty of color.* Westport, CT: Greenwood Press.

Garrison, L. (1941a). Preparation of junior college instructors. *Junior College Journal, 12*(3), 135–141.

Garrison, L. (1941b). Preparation of junior college instructors. *Junior College Journal, 12*(4), 204–209.

Garrison, R. (1967). *Junior college faculty: Issues and problems. A preliminary national appraisal.* Washington, DC: American Association of Junior Colleges.

Glazer-Raymo, J. (1999). *Shattering the myths: Women in academe.* Baltimore: Johns Hopkins University Press.

Grant, M. R., and Keim, M. (2002). Faculty development in publicly supported two-year colleges. *Community College Journal of Research and Practice, 26,* 793–807.

Grubb, W. N. (2005, June 6). Is the tech vs. liberal arts debate out-of-date? Two views. *Community College Week,* pp. 4–5.

Grubb, W. N., and Associates. (1999). *Honored but invisible: An inside look at teaching in community colleges.* New York: Routledge.

Grubb, W. N., Badway, N., and Bell, D. (2003). Community colleges and the equity agenda: The potential of noncredit education. *Annals of the American Academy of Political and Social Science, 586,* 218–240.

Hagedorn, L. S. (2004). *Speaking community college: A glossary of appropriate terms.* Paper presented at the annual meeting of the Council for the Study of Community Colleges, Kansas City, Missouri.

Hagedorn, L. S., and Laden, B. V. (2002). Exploring the climate for women as community college faculty. In C. L. Outcalt (Ed.), *Community college faculty: Characteristics, practices, and challenges* (pp. 69–78). New Directions for Community Colleges, no. 118. San Francisco: Jossey-Bass.

Hammons, J. (1984). The department/division chairperson: Educational leader? *Community and Junior College Journal, 54*(3), 3–7.

Harris, A. A., and Prentice, M. K. (2004). The role exit process of community college faculty: A study of faculty retirement. *Community College Journal of Research and Practice, 28*(9), 729–743.

Hill, E. A. (1986). Job satisfaction facets as predictors of commitment to or withdrawal from the work organization among selected community college faculty in New York State. *Community/Junior College Quarterly of Research and Practice, 10*(1), 1–11.

Hill, M. (1983). Some factors affecting the job satisfaction of community college faculty in Pennsylvania. *Community/Junior College Quarterly of Research and Practice, 7*(4), 303–317.

Horn, L. J., and Nevill, S. (2006). *Profile of undergraduates in U.S. postsecondary education institutions: 2003–04, with a special analysis of community college students.* Washington, DC: National Center for Education Statistics, U.S. Department of Education.

Huber, M. T. (1998). *Community college faculty attitudes and trends, 1997.* Menlo Park, CA: Carnegie Foundation for the Advancement of Teaching.

Hughes, E. (1937). Career and office. *American Journal of Sociology, 43,* 404–413.

Iowa State Education Association. (2005). For members: 2006 legislative agenda. Retrieved July 10, 2006, from http://www.isea.org/members/government-relations/index.htm.

Jacoby, D. (2006). Effects of faculty on community college graduation rates. *Journal of Higher Education, 77*(6), 1081–1103.

Jantzen, J. M., and Cobb, E. G. (1958). A teaching doctorate degree for junior college instructors. *Junior College Journal, 29,* 213–214.

Jencks, C., and Reisman, D. (1969). *The academic revolution.* Garden City, NY: Doubleday & Company.

Keim, M. C. (1989). Two-year college faculty: A research update. *Community College Review, 17*(3), 34–41.

Keim, M. C., and Biletzky, P. E. (1999). Teaching methods used by part-time community college faculty. *Community College Journal of Research and Practice, 23,* 727–737.

Keller, C. (2006). *Faculty counts by category, gender, race/ethnicity.* Unpublished data.

Kelly, D. K. (1990, May 2). Reviving the deadwood: How to create an institutional climate to encourage the professional growth and revitalization of mid-career faculty. Retrieved July 10, 2006, from http://www.tme2lrn.com/index_files/Reviving%20the%20Deadwood.doc.

Koos, L. V. (1947). Junior-college teachers: Degrees and graduate residence. *Junior College Journal, 18*(2), 71–89.

Koos, L. V. (1948a). Junior-college teachers: Background of experience. *Junior College Journal, 18*(8), 457–469.

Koos, L. V. (1948b). Junior-college teachers: Preparation in education. *Junior College Journal, 18*(6), 332–344.

Koos, L. V. (1949). Programs of junior-college teacher preparation. *Junior College Journal, 18,* 423–424.

Kozeracki, C., and Brooks, J. B. (2006). Emerging institutional support for developmental education. In B. Townsend and K. Doughterty (Eds.), *Community college missions in the 21st century* (pp. 63–73). New Directions for Community Colleges. San Francisco: Jossey-Bass.

Lankard, B. A. (1993). *Part-time instructors in adult and vocational education.* ERIC Digest. Columbus, OH: ERIC Clearinghouse on Adult Career and Vocational Education. (ED 363 797)

Larson, M. (1977). *The rise of professionalism*. Berkeley: University of California Press.

Levin, J. S., Kater, S., and Wagoner, R. L. (2006). *Community college faculty: At work in the new economy.* New York: Palgrave Macmillan.

Locke, E. A., Fitzpatrick, W., and White, F. M. (1983). Job satisfaction and role clarity among university and college faculty. *Review of Higher Education, 6*(4), 343–365.

London, H. (1978). *Culture of a community college.* New York: Praeger.

Lucey, C. A. (2002). Civic engagement, shared governance, and community colleges. *Academe, 88*(4), 27–31.

Manzo, K. K. (2000). Community college faculty. *Black Issues in Higher Education, 17*(13), 54–57.

McBride, S. A., Munday, R. G., and Tunnell, J. (1992). Community college job satisfaction and propensity to leave. *Community/Junior College Quarterly of Research and Practice, 16*(2), 157–165.

McGrath, D., and Spear, M. B. (1991). *The academic crisis of the community college.* Albany: State University of New York Press.

Miller, M. (2003). The status of faculty senates in community colleges. *Community College Journal of Research and Practice, 27,* 419–428.

Monroe, C. (1977). *Profile of the community college: A handbook.* San Francisco: Jossey-Bass.

Murray, J. (1995). Faculty (mis)development in Ohio 2-year colleges. *Community College Journal of Research and Practice, 19*(6), 549–563.

Murray, J. (1999a). Faculty development in a national sample of community colleges. *Community College Review, 27*(3), 47–64.

Murray, J. (1999b). Interviewing to hire competent community college faculty. *Community College Review, 27*(1), 41–56.

Murray, J. (2000). Faculty development in Texas two-year colleges. *Community College Journal of Research and Practice, 24,* 251–267.

Murray, J. (2001). Faculty development in publicly supported 2-year colleges. *Community College Journal of Research and Practice, 25,* 487–502.

Murray, J. (2002). Faculty development in SACS-accredited community colleges. *Community College Review, 29*(4), 50–66.

National Center for Postsecondary Improvement. (1998, November/December). Casting new light on old notions: A changing understanding of community college faculty. *Change,* pp. 43–46.

Olson, S. J., Jensrud, Q., and McCann, P. L. (2001). Preparation and credentialing requirements of two-year college technical instructors: A national study. *Journal of Industrial Teacher Education, 38*(2). Retrieved July 7, 2006, from http://scholar.lib.vt.edu/ejournals/JITE/v38n2/olson.html.

Opp, R. D., and Gosetti, P. (2002). Women full-time faculty of color in 2-year colleges: A trend and predictive analysis. *Community College Journal of Research and Practice, 26*(7–8), 609–627.

Opp, R. D., and Smith, A. (1994). Effective strategies for enhancing minority faculty recruitment and retention. In W. B. Harvey and J. Valadez (Eds.), *Creating and maintaining a diverse faculty* (pp. 43–56). New Directions for Community Colleges, no. 87. San Francisco: Jossey-Bass.

Outcalt, C. L. (Ed.). (2002a). *Community college faculty: Characteristics, practices, and challenges.* New Directions for Community Colleges, no. 118. San Francisco: Jossey-Bass.

Outcalt, C. L. (Ed.). (2002b). *A profile of the community college professorate, 1975–2000.* New York: Routledge Falmer Press.

Owens, J. S., Reis, F. W., and Hall, K. M. (1994). *Bridging the gap: Recruitment and retention of minority faculty members* (pp. 57–64). New Directions for Community Colleges, no. 87. San Francisco: Jossey-Bass.

Palmer, J. C. (1991). Nurturing scholarship at community colleges. In G. B. Vaughan and J. C. Palmer (Eds.), *Enhancing teaching and administration through scholarship* (pp. 69–77). New Directions for Community Colleges, no. 76. San Francisco: Jossey-Bass.

Palmer, J. C. (1992). Faculty professionalism reconsidered. In K. Kroll (Ed.), *Maintaining faculty excellence* (pp. 29–38). New Directions for Community Colleges, no. 79. San Francisco: Jossey-Bass.

Palmer, J. C. (1999). Faculty at community colleges: A national profile. In *NEA 1999 Almanac of Higher Education* (pp. 45–53). Washington, DC: National Education Association.

Palmer, J. C. (2002). Disciplinary variations in the work of full-time faculty. In C. L. Outcalt (Ed.), *Community college faculty: Characteristics, practices, and challenges* (pp. 9–20). New Directions for Community Colleges, no. 118. San Francisco: Jossey-Bass.

Parsad, B., and Lewis, L. (2003). *Remedial education at degree-granting postsecondary institutions in fall 2000: Statistical analysis report.* No. 2004–010. Washington, DC: National Center for Education Statistics, U.S. Department of Education.

Pascarella, E. T., and others. (1998). Does community college versus four-year college attendance influence students' educational plans? *Journal of College Student Development, 39*(2), 179–193.

Perin, D. (2002). The location of developmental education in community colleges: A discussion of the merits of mainstreaming vs. centralization. *Community College Review, 30*(4), 21–46.

Perna, L. W. (2003). The status of women and minorities among community college faculty. *Research in Higher Education, 44*(2), 205–240.

Pope, M., and Miller, M. (2000). Community college faculty governance leaders: Results of a national survey. *Community College Journal of Research and Practice, 24,* 627–638.

Prager, C. (2003). Scholarship matters. *Community/Junior College Quarterly of Research and Practice, 27,* 579–592.

Rafes, R., and Warren, E. (2001). Hiring and firing in community colleges: Caveats and considerations for protecting institutions and employees. *Community College Journal of Research and Practice, 25,* 283–296.

Redmon, K. D. (1999). Faculty evaluation: A response to competing values. *Community College Review, 27*(1), 57–71.

Rhoades, G. (1998). *Managed professionals: Unionized faculty and restructuring academic labor.* Albany: State University of New York Press.

Rifkin, T. (2000). *Public community college faculty.* New Expeditions Issues, no. 4. Washington, DC: Community College Press.

Rosser, V. J., and Townsend, B. K. (2006). Determining public 2-year college faculty's intent to leave: An empirical model. *Journal of Higher Education, 77*(1), 124–147.

Roueche, J. E., Roueche, S. D., and Milliron, M. D. (1995). *Strangers in their own land: Part-time faculty in American community colleges.* Washington, DC: Community College Press.

Rubiales, D. (1998). Collective bargaining at community colleges: A report from California. *Academe, 84*(6), 40–42.

Rudolph, F. (1977). *Curriculum: A history of the American undergraduate course of study since 1636.* San Francisco: Jossey-Bass.

Russo, S. (1938). Qualifications of the junior college faculty. *Junior College Journal, 8*(4), 193–194.

St. Petersburg College. (2006). *Baccalaureate program.* Retrieved September 9, 2006, from http://www.spcollege.edu/bachelors/program.php.

Schuetz, P. (2002). Instructional practices of part-time and full-time faculty. In C. L. Outcalt (Ed.), *Community college faculty: Characteristics, practices, and challenges* (pp. 17–25). New Directions for Community Colleges, no. 118. San Francisco: Jossey-Bass.

Schuster, J. H., and Finkelstein, M. J. (2006). *The American faculty: The restructuring of academic work and careers.* Baltimore: Johns Hopkins University Press.

Seagren, A., and others. (1994). *Academic leadership in community colleges.* Lincoln: University of Nebraska Press.

Seidman, E. (1985). *In the words of the faculty.* San Francisco: Jossey-Bass.

Shapiro, C. (1964). In defense of the publishing teacher. *AACJC Journal, 34*(6), 28–29.

Sheldon, C. Q. (2002, October). *Building an instructional framework for effective community college developmental education.* ERIC Clearinghouse for Community Colleges. (EDO-JC-02-09)

Spear, M., Seymour, E., and McGrath, D. (1992). The new problem of staff development. In K. Kroll (Ed.), *Maintaining faculty excellence* (pp. 21–28). New Directions for Community Colleges, no. 79. San Francisco: Jossey-Bass.

Sydow, D. (2000). Long-term investment in professional development: Real dividends in teaching and learning. *Community College Journal of Research and Practice, 24,* 383–397.

Thaxter, L., and Graham, S. (1999). Community college faculty involvement in decision-making. *Community College Journal of Research and Practice, 23,* 655–674.

Tierney, W. G. (Ed.). (2004). *Competing conceptions of academic governance: Negotiating the perfect storm.* Baltimore: Johns Hopkins University Press.

Tierney, W. G., and Bensimon, E. M. (1996). *Promotion and tenure: Community and socialization in academe.* Albany: State University of New York Press.

Tillery, D. (1963). Academic rank: Promise or peril? *AACJC Journal, 33*(6), 6–9.

Townsend, B. K. (Ed.). (1995). Women community college faculty: On the margins or in the mainstream? In B. K. Townsend (Ed.), *Gender and power in the community college* (pp. 39–46). New Directions for Community Colleges, no. 89. San Francisco: Jossey-Bass.

Townsend, B. K. (1998). Women faculty: Satisfaction with employment in the community college. *Community College Journal of Research and Practice, 22,* 655–662.

Townsend, B. K. (Ed.). (1999). *Understanding the impact of reverse transfer students on community colleges.* New Directions for Community Colleges, no. 106. San Francisco: Jossey-Bass.

Townsend, B. K. (2001). Redefining the community college transfer mission. *Community College Review, 29*(2), 29–42.

Townsend, B. K. (2004, November). *The upside-down degree.* Paper presented in Democratization or destruction of the baccalaureate? The upside-down degree and the community college baccalaureate. Symposium conducted at annual meeting of Association for the Study of Higher Education, Kansas City, Missouri.

Townsend, B. K. (2006, November). *Blurring institutional types: The authorization of community colleges to award the baccalaureate degree.* Paper presented at the annual meeting of the Association for the Study of Higher Education, Anaheim, CA.

Townsend, B. K., and LaPaglia, N. (2000). Are we marginalized within academe? Perceptions of two-year college faculty. *Community College Review, 28*(1), 41–48.

Townsend, B. K., and Twombly, S. (forthcoming). Accidental equity: The status of women in the community college. *Equity and Excellence in Education.*

Truell, A. D., Price, W. T., and Joyner, R. L. (1998). Job satisfaction among community college occupational-technical faculty. *Community College Journal of Research and Practice, 22*(2), 111–122.

Twombly, S. (2005). Values, policies, and practices affecting the hiring process for full-time arts and sciences faculty in community colleges. *Journal of Higher Education, 76*(4), 423–447.

U.S. Department of Education. (2005). *Digest of education statistics: 2005.* Table 230. Washington, DC: National Center for Education Statistics.

U.S. Department of Education. (2006). *A test of leadership: Charting the future of U.S. higher education.* Spellings Commission report. Washington, DC: U.S. Department of Education. Retrieved January 8, 2007, from http://www.ed.gov/about/bdscomm/list/hiedfuture/reports/pre-pub-report.pdf.

Valadez, J. R., and Antony, J. S. (2001). Job satisfaction and commitment of two-year college part-time faculty. *Community College Journal of Research and Practice, 25,* 97–108.

VanDerLinden, K. (2002). *Credit student analysis: 1999 and 2000.* Washington, DC: American Association of Community Colleges, and Ames, IA: ACT, Inc.

Vaughan, G. B. (1986). In pursuit of scholarship. *AACJC Journal, 56*(4), 12–16.

Vaughan, G. B. (1988). Scholarship in the community colleges: Path to respect. *Educational Record, 69,* 217–237.

Vaughan, G. B. (1992). The community college unbound. In *Prisoners of elitism: The community college's struggle for stature* (pp. 23–34). New Directions for Community Colleges, no. 78, San Francisco: Jossey-Bass.

Walker, K. (2001). Opening the door to the baccalaureate degree. *Community College Review, 29*(2), 18–28.

Walker, K. (2006, June/July). Globalization is changing the world of education: A case for the community college baccalaureate. *Community College Journal,* 14–19.

Wallace, S. (1999, June/July). Meeting the needs of information-age employers. *Community College Journal, 69*(6), 10–12.

Wallin, D. L. (2004). Valuing professional colleagues: Part-time faculty in community and technical colleges. *Community College Journal of Research and Practice, 28,* 373–391.

Wattenbarger, J. (2000). Colleges should stick to what they do best. *Community College Week, 13*(18), 4–5.

West Virginia Higher Education Policy Commission Meeting Agenda. (2001, June 29). Retrieved July 10, 2006, from http://www.hepc.wvnet.edu/commission/Agenda_June_2001.pdf.

Winter, P. (1996). The application of marketing theory to community college faculty recruitment: An empirical test. *Community College Review, 24,* 3–16.

Winter, P., and Kjorlien, C. (2000a). Community college faculty recruitment: Effects of job mobility, recruiter similarity-dissimilarity, and applicant gender. *Community College Journal of Research and Practice, 24,* 547–566.

Winter, P., and Kjorlien, C. (2000b). Community college faculty recruitment: Predictors of applicant attraction to faculty positions. *Community College Review, 28*(1), 23–40.

Winter, P., and Kjorlien, C. (2001). Business faculty recruitment: The effects of full-time versus part-time employment. *Community College Review, 29*(1), 18–34.

Wolf-Wendel, L., Ward, K., and Twombly, S. (2007). Faculty life at community colleges: The perspective of women with children. *Community College Review, 34*(4), 255–281.

Wolfe, J. R., and Strange, C. C. (2003). Academic life at the franchise: Faculty culture in a rural two-year branch campus. *Review of Higher Education, 26*(3), 343–362.

Name Index

A

Abbott, A., 105, 106
Adelman, C., 36
Alfred, R., 86–88
Amey, M., 70, 71, 73, 75, 115
Angelo, T. A., 39
Antony, J. S., 27, 28, 51, 52
Avakian, A. N., 24, 41

B

Badway, N., 21, 22
Bayer, A. E., 110, 111, 140
Bell, D., 21, 22
Bensimon, E. M., 134
Berger, A., 24
Biletzky, P. E., 26
Blocker, C. E., 74
Boggs, G., 1
Bowen, H., 4
Bower, B. L., 13
Boyer, E., 11, 38–40, 54, 130
Bradburn, E. M., 11, 12, 14, 24, 27, 56, 75, 79
Brawer, F., 5, 6, 18, 20, 21, 42, 43, 60–65, 75, 79, 88, 89, 93, 99, 107, 108, 110, 111, 113, 114, 129, 131
Braxton, J. M., 110, 111, 140
Brewer, D. J., 22
Brooks, J. B., 22
Burgess, L. A., 26
Burke, T. R., 119
Burnstad, H. M., 43, 47

C

Campion, W. J., 77
Caplow, T., 2, 127
Case, C., 88
Cataldi, E., 11, 12, 14, 24, 27, 56, 75, 79
Cheslock, J., 60, 62
Clark, B., 2, 4, 61, 85, 86, 108, 112–115, 129
Cobb, E. G., 57, 58
Cohen, A., 5, 6, 18, 20, 21, 42, 43, 60–65, 75, 79, 88, 89, 93, 99, 107–111, 113, 114, 129, 131
Collins, L., 75, 94, 95, 97
Colvert, C. C., 57, 58
Cooper, T. L., 134
Cross, K. P., 39
Cunningham, J. D., 88
Curtis, J. W., 79

D

Dee, J. R., 79
Deegan, W., 88
Diaz, V., 60, 62
Dickinson, R., 25
Dobrovolny, J. S., 57
Dolan, F. H., 57, 58, 65

E

Eaton, J. S., 120
Eckert, R. E., 57, 58
Eells, W. C., 57
Erdman, H., 77

Subject Index

A
Academic ability, 35
*Academic Life: Small Worlds, Different
Worlds* (Clark), 2–4, 112
Academic Senate for California
Community Colleges, 95
Age
of full-time faculty, 18
of part-time faculty, 27–28
of students, 36
American Association of Community
Colleges, 1, 6, 57
American Association of University
Professors (AAUP), 28, 79, 89, 95
American Community College (Cohen and
Brawer), 5, 6
*American Faculty: The Restructuring of
Academic Work and Careers* (Schuster
and Finkelstein), 4
American Federation of Teachers, 89
*American Professors: A Natural Resource
Imperiled* (Bowen and Schuster), 4
Arkansas, 120
Associate of Applied Science, 34,
121–123
Associate of Arts degree, 33, 34
Austin Community College, 47

C
California, 7, 19, 75, 95, 97
California Assembly Bill 1725, 94, 95
Career
dimensions of, 55–83

entry requirements for, 59–68
other requirements for, 67–68
preparation for, 56–59
and prior employment, 63–67
stages, 72–81
Carnegie Foundation, 50
Carnegie survey, 7
Center for the Study of Community
Colleges, 26
Central Oregon Community College, 76
Chronicle of Higher Education Almanac, 11,
12, 69
Collective bargaining, 88–94
and retrenchment and reorganization,
91–94
and rewards, 90–91
College of the Canyons (California), 49
Colorado, 77
Community College Baccalaureate,
118–122
Community College Baccalaureate
Association, 118, 119
Community College faculty
career dimensions of, 11–31
challenges in understanding,
132–138
fresh look at, 127–132
full-time, 11–24
overview, 1–9
part-time, 24–30
preparation to become, 56–59
profile of, 11–31
work of, 33–54

Missions, community college, 33–37
Missouri, 118
Missouri Southern State University, 118
Missouri Western State University, 118

N

National Center for Education Statistics (NCES), 18, 24, 28, 60
National Center for Postsecondary Improvement, 1
National Education Association (NEA), 89
National Postsecondary Student Aid Study, 34
National Study of Postsecondary Faculty (NSOPF), 6–7, 11, 16–18, 21, 23, 25, 26, 28, 37, 38, 41, 50–52, 62, 63, 65, 66, 74, 75, 78, 80, 89
National Survey of Faculty (Carnegie Foundation), 50
National Survey of Postsecondary Faculty, 8
NCES. *See* National Center for Education Statistics
New York State, 19
North Carolina, 79
North Central Association of Colleges and Schools, 51, 90, 93
Nouveau College, 116, 118–122
NSOPF. *See* National Study of Postsecondary Faculty

O

Ohio, 43, 45

P

Part-time faculty, 24–30
  age of, 27
  educational credentials of, 27–28
  gender and race or ethnicity of, 26–27
  professional development for, 48–49
  salaries of, 28–30
Preparation, 56–59
Preparing Future Faculty program, 109
Prince George's Community College (Largo, Maryland), 13
Professional development, 41–49
  activities, 43–44

components of, programs, 43
  institutional support for, 44–48
  for part-time faculty, 48–49
Professional Development Initiative (PDI), 47
Professionalization
  and characteristics of profession, 105–107
  and community college teaching as profession, 107–117
  possible future influences on, 118–124
  and status of community college teaching as profession, 105–125
Profile of the Community College Professoriate, 1975–2000 (Outcalt), 4, 132
Promotion, 74–77, 134–135

R

Race: of full-time faculty, 11–13; of part-time faculty, 26–27
Rank, academic, 73–74
Recruitment, 69–71
Reorganization, 91–94
Requirements, entry, 59–68
Research, full-time faculty, 38–40
Retention, faculty, 79–80
Retirement, 80–81
Retrenchment, 91–94
Role expectations
  for full-time faculty, 37–41
  for part-time faculty, 41

S

SACS. *See* Southern Association of Colleges and Schools
Salaries
  determination of, 77–79
  of full-time faculty, 23–24
  of part-time faculty, 28–30
Scholarship, full-time faculty, 38–40
Search process, 68–72
  and bases for hiring decisions, 72
  and nature of interview, 71–72
  and recruitment, 69–71
Service, 40–41

About the Authors

Barbara K. Townsend is professor of higher education and director of the Center for Community College Research at the University of Missouri–Columbia. Her current research focuses on access to and attainment of the baccalaureate, particularly through the transfer function and especially for women and minorities.

Susan B. Twombly is professor of higher education and chair of the Department of Educational Leadership and Policy Studies at the University of Kansas. Her current research interests include postsecondary faculty, particularly community college faculty, gender in higher education, and higher education in Latin America.

About the ASHE Higher Education Report Series

Since 1983, the ASHE (formerly ASHE-ERIC) Higher Education Report Series has been providing researchers, scholars, and practitioners with timely and substantive information on the critical issues facing higher education. Each monograph presents a definitive analysis of a higher education problem or issue, based on a thorough synthesis of significant literature and institutional experiences. Topics range from planning to diversity and multiculturalism, to performance indicators, to curricular innovations. The mission of the Series is to link the best of higher education research and practice to inform decision making and policy. The reports connect conventional wisdom with research and are designed to help busy individuals keep up with the higher education literature. Authors are scholars and practitioners in the academic community. Each report includes an executive summary, review of the pertinent literature, descriptions of effective educational practices, and a summary of key issues to keep in mind to improve educational policies and practice.

The Series is one of the most peer reviewed in higher education. A National Advisory Board made up of ASHE members reviews proposals. A National Review Board of ASHE scholars and practitioners reviews completed manuscripts. Six monographs are published each year and they are approximately 120 pages in length. The reports are widely disseminated through Jossey-Bass and John Wiley & Sons, and they are available online to subscribing institutions through Wiley InterScience (http://www.interscience.wiley.com).

Call for Proposals

The ASHE Higher Education Report Series is actively looking for proposals. We encourage you to contact one of the editors, Dr. Kelly Ward (kaward@wsu.edu) or Dr. Lisa Wolf-Wendel (lwolf@ku.edu), with your ideas.

Recent Titles

ASHE HIGHER EDUCATION REPORT
Order Form
SUBSCRIPTIONS AND SINGLE ISSUES

DISCOUNTED BACK ISSUES:

*Use this form to receive **20% off** all back issues of ASHE Higher Education Report. All single issues priced at **$22.40** (normally $28.00)*

TITLE	ISSUE NO.	ISBN
_____	_____	_____
_____	_____	_____

Call 888-378-2537 *or see mailing instructions below. When calling, mention the promotional code, JB7ND, to receive your discount.*

SUBSCRIPTIONS: *(1 year, 6 issues)*

☐ New Order   ☐ Renewal

U.S.	☐ Individual: $165	☐ Institutional: $199
Canada/Mexico	☐ Individual: $165	☐ Institutional: $235
All Others	☐ Individual: $201	☐ Institutional: $310

Call 888-378-2537 *or see mailing and pricing instructions below. Online subscriptions are available at www.interscience.wiley.com.*

Copy or detach page and send to:
John Wiley & Sons, Journals Dept., 5th Floor
989 Market Street, San Francisco, CA 94103-1741

Order Form can also be faxed to: 888-481-2665

Issue/Subscription Amount: $ _____

Shipping Amount: $ _____
(for single issues only—subscription prices include shipping)

Total Amount: $ _____

SHIPPING CHARGES:		
SURFACE	Domestic	Canadian
First Item	$5.00	$6.00
Each Add'l Item	$3.00	$1.50

(No sales tax for U.S. subscriptions. Canadian residents, add GST for subscription orders. Individual rate subscriptions must be paid by personal check or credit card. Individual rate subscriptions may not be resold as library copies.)

☐ Payment enclosed (U.S. check or money order only. All payments must be in U.S. dollars.)

☐ VISA ☐ MC ☐ Amex # _____ Exp. Date _____

Card Holder Name _____ Card Issue # _____

Signature_____ Day Phone _____

☐ Bill Me (U.S. institutional orders only. Purchase order required.)

Purchase order # _____
Federal Tax ID13559302   GST 89102 8052

Name_____
Address _____
Phone _____ E-mail _____

JB7ND

**ASHE-ERIC HIGHER EDUCATION REPORT
IS NOW AVAILABLE ONLINE AT WILEY INTERSCIENCE**

What is Wiley InterScience?

Wiley InterScience is the dynamic online content service from John Wiley & Sons delivering the full text of over 300 leading scientific, technical, medical, and professional journals, plus major reference works, the acclaimed Current Protocols laboratory manuals, and even the full text of select Wiley print books online.

What are some special features of Wiley InterScience?

Wiley Interscience Alerts is a service that delivers table of contents via e-mail for any journal available on Wiley InterScience as soon as a new issue is published online.
Early View is Wiley's exclusive service presenting individual articles online as soon as they are ready, even before the release of the compiled print issue. These articles are complete, peer-reviewed, and citable.
CrossRef is the innovative multi-publisher reference linking system enabling readers to move seamlessly from a reference in a journal article to the cited publication, typically located on a different server and published by a different publisher.

How can I access Wiley InterScience?

Visit http://www.interscience.wiley.com.

Guest Users can browse Wiley InterScience for unrestricted access to journal Tables of Contents and Article Abstracts, or use the powerful search engine.
Registered Users are provided with a *Personal Home Page* to store and manage customized alerts, searches, and links to favorite journals and articles. Additionally, Registered Users can view free Online Sample Issues and preview selected material from major reference works.
Licensed Customers are entitled to access full-text journal articles in PDF, with select journals also offering full-text HTML.

How do I become an Authorized User?

Authorized Users are individuals authorized by a paying Customer to have access to the journals in Wiley InterScience. For example, a University that subscribes to Wiley journals is considered to be the Customer.
Faculty, staff and students authorized by the University to have access to those journals in Wiley InterScience are Authorized Users. Users should contact their Library for information on which Wiley journals they have access to in Wiley InterScience.

ASK YOUR INSTITUTION ABOUT WILEY INTERSCIENCE TODAY!